Oxford AQA GCSE History

Power and the People

c1170–Present Day

AUTHORS

Lindsay Bruce

Aaron Wilkes

SERIES EDITOR

Aaron Wilkes

CONSULTANT

J. A. Cloake

OXFORD
UNIVERSITY PRESS

OXFORD
UNIVERSITY PRESS

Great Clarendon Street, Oxford, OX2 6DP, United Kingdom

Oxford University Press is a department of the University of Oxford.

It furthers the University's objective of excellence in research, scholarship, and education by publishing worldwide. Oxford is a registered trade mark of Oxford University Press in the UK and in certain other countries.

First published in 2021

British Library Cataloguing in Publication Data

Data available

978-138-202313-9

Digital edition 978-138-202314-6

1 3 5 7 9 10 8 6 4 2

Paper used in the production of this book is a natural, recyclable product made from wood grown in sustainable forests.

The manufacturing process conforms to the environmental regulations of the country of origin.

Printed and bound by CPI Group (UK) Ltd, Croydon, CR0 4YY

Approval message from AQA

This textbook has been approved by AQA for use with our qualification. This means that we have checked that it broadly covers the specification and we are satisfied with the overall quality. Full details of our approval process can be found on our website.

We approve textbooks because we know how important it is for teachers and students to have the right resources to support their teaching and learning. However, the publisher is ultimately responsible for the editorial control and quality of this book.

Please note that when teaching the AQA GCSE History course, you must refer to AQA's specification as your definitive source of information. While this book has been written to match the specification, it cannot provide complete coverage of every aspect of the course.
A wide range of other useful resources can be found on the relevant subject pages of our website: www.aqa.org.uk.

The publisher would like to thank Jon Cloake for his work on the first edition of the Student Book on which this second edition is based. The publisher would also like to thank Chris Edge, Ben Fuller (Holocaust Educational Trust) and David Rawlings for their contribution in the development of this book.

Contents

Power and the People c1170–Present Day

Introduction to the Oxford AQA GCSE History series

The Oxford AQA GCSE History series has been specially written by an expert team of teachers and historians with examining experience to match each part of your AQA course. The chapters which follow are laid out according to the content of the AQA specification. Written in an interesting and engaging style, each of the eye-catching double-pages is clearly organised to provide you with a logical route through the historical content.

There is a lively mix of visual **Sources** and **Interpretations** to enhance and challenge your learning and understanding of the history. Extensive use of photographs, diagrams, cartoons, charts and maps allows you to practise using a variety of sources as evidence.

The **Work** activities and **Practice Questions** have been written to help you check your understanding of the content, develop your skills as a historian, and help you prepare not just for GCSE examinations, but for any future studies. You can develop your knowledge and practise examination skills further through the interactive activities, history skills animations, practice questions, revision checklists and more on *Kerboodle**.

Thematic Studies

This book guides you through one of AQA's Thematic Studies, Britain: Power and the People c1170–Present Day. Thematic studies focus on key developments in the history of Britain over a long period of time. You will look at the importance of factors such as war, religion, government, communication, ideas and the role of the individual, and how these factors impact upon society.

Understanding history requires not just knowledge, but also a good grasp of concepts such as causation, consequence and change. This book is designed to help you think historically, and features primary sources; these sources will help you think about how historians base their understanding on the careful evaluation of evidence from the past.

We hope you'll enjoy your study of Power and the People –

Jon Cloake
Series Consultant

Aaron Wilkes
Series Editor

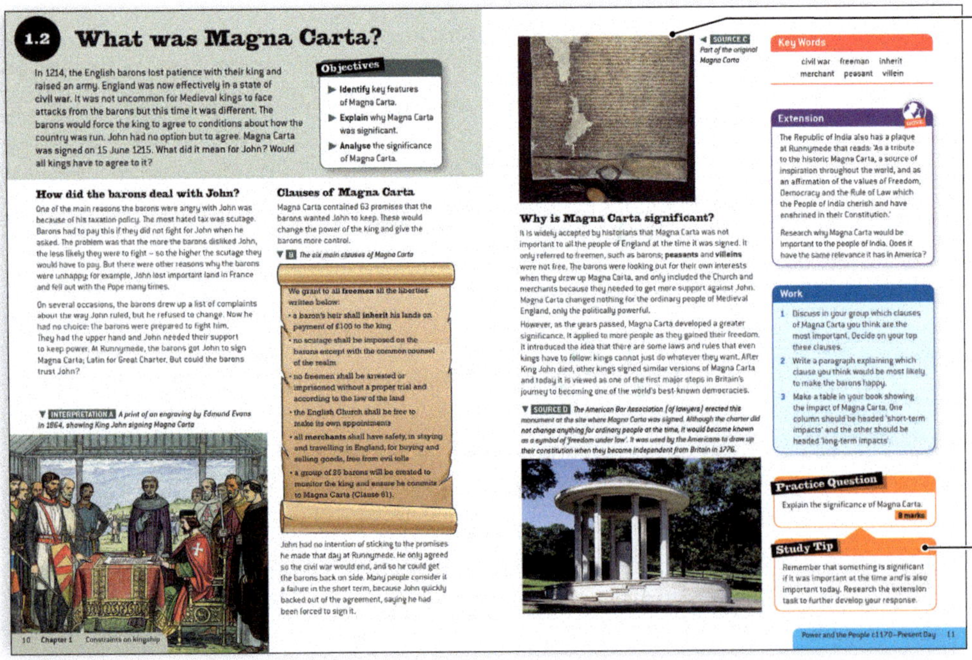

1.2 What was Magna Carta?

In 1214, the English barons lost patience with their king and raised an army. England was now effectively in a state of civil war. It was not uncommon for Medieval kings to face attacks from the barons but this time it was different. The barons would force the king to agree to conditions about how the country was run. John had no option but to agree. Magna Carta was signed on 15 June 1215. What did it mean for John? Would all kings have to agree to it?

Objectives
- **Identify** key features of Magna Carta.
- **Explain** why Magna Carta was significant.
- **Analyse** the significance of Magna Carta.

How did the barons deal with John?

One of the main reasons the barons were angry with John was because of his taxation policy. The most hated tax was scutage. Barons had to pay this if they did not fight for John when he asked. The problem was that the more the barons disliked John, the less likely they were to fight – so the higher the scutage they would have to pay. But there were other reasons why the barons were unhappy; for example, John lost important land in France and fell out with the Pope many times.

On several occasions, the barons drew up a list of complaints about the way John ruled, but he refused to change. Now he had no choice: the barons were prepared to fight him. They had the upper hand and John needed their support to keep power. At Runnymede, the barons got John to sign Magna Carta; Latin for Great Charter. But could the barons trust John?

INTERPRETATION A *A print of an engraving by Edmund Evans in 1864, showing King John signing Magna Carta*

Clauses of Magna Carta

Magna Carta contained 63 promises that the barons wanted John to keep. These would change the power of the king and give the barons more control.

B *The six main clauses of Magna Carta*

We grant to all **freemen** all the liberties written below:
- a baron's heir shall **inherit** his lands on payment of £100 to the king
- no scutage shall be imposed on the barons except with the common counsel of the realm
- no freemen shall be arrested or imprisoned without a proper trial and according to the law of the land
- the English Church shall be free to make its own appointments
- all **merchants** shall have safety in staying and travelling in England, for buying and selling goods, free from evil tolls
- a group of 25 barons will be created to monitor the king and ensure he commits to Magna Carta (Clause 61).

John had no intention of sticking to the promises he made that day at Runnymede. He only agreed so the civil war would end, and so he could get the barons back on side. Many people consider it a failure in the short term, because John quickly backed out of the agreement, saying he had been forced to sign it.

10 Chapter 1 Constraints on kingship

SOURCE C *Part of the original Magna Carta*

Why is Magna Carta significant?

It is widely accepted by historians that Magna Carta was not important to all the people of England at the time it was signed. It only referred to freemen, such as barons; **peasants** and **villeins** were not free. The barons were looking out for their own interests when they drew up Magna Carta, and only included the Church and merchants because they needed to get more support against John. Magna Carta changed nothing for the ordinary people of Medieval England, only the politically powerful.

However, as the years passed, Magna Carta developed a greater significance. It applied to more people as they gained their freedom. It introduced the idea that there are some laws and rules that even kings have to follow: kings cannot just do whatever they want. After King John died, other kings signed similar versions of Magna Carta and today it is viewed as one of the first major steps in Britain's journey to becoming one of the world's best-known democracies.

SOURCE D *The American Bar Association (of lawyers) erected this monument at the site where Magna Carta was signed. Although the charter did not change anything for ordinary people at the time, it would become known as a symbol of 'freedom under law'. It was used by the Americans to draw up their constitution when they became independent from Britain in 1776.*

Key Words

civil war freeman inherit merchant peasant villein

Extension

The Republic of India also has a plaque at Runnymede that reads: 'As a tribute to the historic Magna Carta, a source of inspiration throughout the world, and as an affirmation of the values of Freedom, Democracy and the Rule of Law which the People of India cherish and have enshrined in their Constitution.'

Research why Magna Carta would be important to the people of India. Does it have the same relevance it has in America?

Work

1. Discuss in your group which clauses of Magna Carta you think are the most important. Decide on your top three clauses.
2. Write a paragraph explaining which clause you think would be most likely to make the barons happy.
3. Make a table in your book showing the impact of Magna Carta. One column should be headed 'short-term impacts' and the other should be headed 'long-term impacts'.

Practice Question

Explain the significance of Magna Carta.
8 marks

Study Tip

Remember that something is significant if it was important at the time *and* is also important today. Research the extension task to further develop your response.

Power and the People c1170–Present Day 11

Sources provide opportunities for you to assess the usefulness of texts or images that are primary or contemporary to the period.

Practice Questions and Study Tips help familiarise you with new-style exam questions.

**Kerboodle* is not approved by AQA.

How to use this book

Written for the new AQA specification, the features in this book include:

Objectives

At the beginning of the sections, you will find a list of learning objectives. These are based on the requirements of the course.

Work

The activities and questions aim to develop your knowledge, understanding and key history skills. They are designed to be progressive in terms of difficulty, and to get you to think about the topic, become familiar with the history, and apply what you have learned.

▼ SOURCE ▼ INTERPRETATION

Sources introduce you to material that is primary or contemporary to the period, and **Interpretations** provide you with various people's different perspectives on the past.

Extension

GCSE

This is an opportunity to challenge you to investigate the history more deeply through independent research and reflection.

Practice Question

These are focused questions to help you practise your history skills, including evaluating sources and essay writing. They give you an idea of the types of questions you might get in an examination.

Key Words

The important phrases and terms are highlighted and are also defined in the glossary. Learn what they mean – and how to spell and use them correctly.

Study Tip

These are hints to highlight key parts of **Practice Questions** and will help you answer the questions.

Timeline

A short list of dates identifying key events to help you understand chronological developments.

Fact

Fascinating references, facts or anecdotes that will make you think and add to your knowledge and understanding.

Key Biography

Details of a key person to help you understand the individuals who have helped shape history.

Timeline

Britain: Power and the People

This thematic study covers over 800 years in the history of the relationship between the citizen and the state in Britain. Beginning in the twelfth century, you will explore how the power and authority of different kings and parliament have been challenged. By examining the journey from feudalism to democracy and equality, you will discover how, in different periods, the state has responded to challenges to its authority and the impact of this.

You will explore how the balance of power changed, why change happened when it did, whether change brought progress, and the significance of the changes. You will also consider how factors – such as war, chance, religion and the economy – sometimes worked together to bring about particular changes at a particular time.

And although the focus of this study is the development of the relationship between power and the people in Britain, it will show how ideas, events or developments in the wider world affected the course of Britain's political development.

1200

1215
Magna Carta is signed by King John

1265
Simon de Montfort calls a parliament that has 'commoners' in it

1300

1381
Local uprisings lead to the Peasants' Revolt; the leader, Wat Tyler, is killed

1500

1536–37
People from the north of England start a pilgrimage to protest about King Henry VIII's changes to the Church

1600

1642–51
English Civil War occurs between those who support King Charles I and those who support parliament

1700

1775–82
Britain's defeat in the War of Independence results in the loss of the American colonies

1800

1804
Toussaint L'Ouverture leads a rebellion against slavery; the new independent island of Haiti is created

1819
The Peterloo Massacre: protestors demanding the vote are attacked by the authorities

1833
Factory Reform Act reduces the amount of hours women and children can work

1834
Tolpuddle Martyrs are arrested for holding a union meeting

1838–48
Chartism movement tries to secure more representation for the working class

1897
The National Union of Women's Suffrage Societies is set up; the campaign for women's suffrage becomes organised

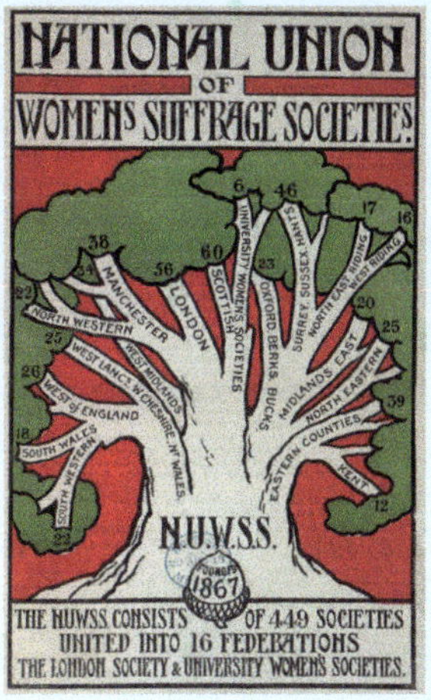

1900

1918
Women over 28 get the vote

1926
General Strike takes place in support of British miners

1948
Empire Windrush arrives in Britain, beginning a new period of migration from Caribbean countries

1981
Brixton Riots take place and lead to the Scarman Report into institutional racism in the police

2000

1.1 What did people want from the Medieval King John?

This topic focuses on the topic of power and its impact on Britain and Britain's people from 1170 to the present day. To understand the topic, you will need to explore how power has been challenged and enforced over the centuries. To begin you will need to understand what Medieval kings were like in Britain, starting with King John. When John became king in 1199 he had a lot to live up to. His father, Henry II, was viewed as a successful king, and his brother was Richard the Lionheart. Richard was a fantastic soldier who had captured and controlled land in France and fought in a **crusade**. A Medieval king was expected to defend his people by leading his army well and maintaining the support of important people in the kingdom, such as the **barons**. He should also keep the country peaceful, successfully deal with rebellions, and try to maintain good relations with the Church. So, did King John have what it took to be a good king?

Objectives

- **Outline** the qualities of a good Medieval king.
- **Explain** why King John was unpopular.
- **Analyse** interpretations of King John and come to a judgement.

▼ **A** *King John's family tree*

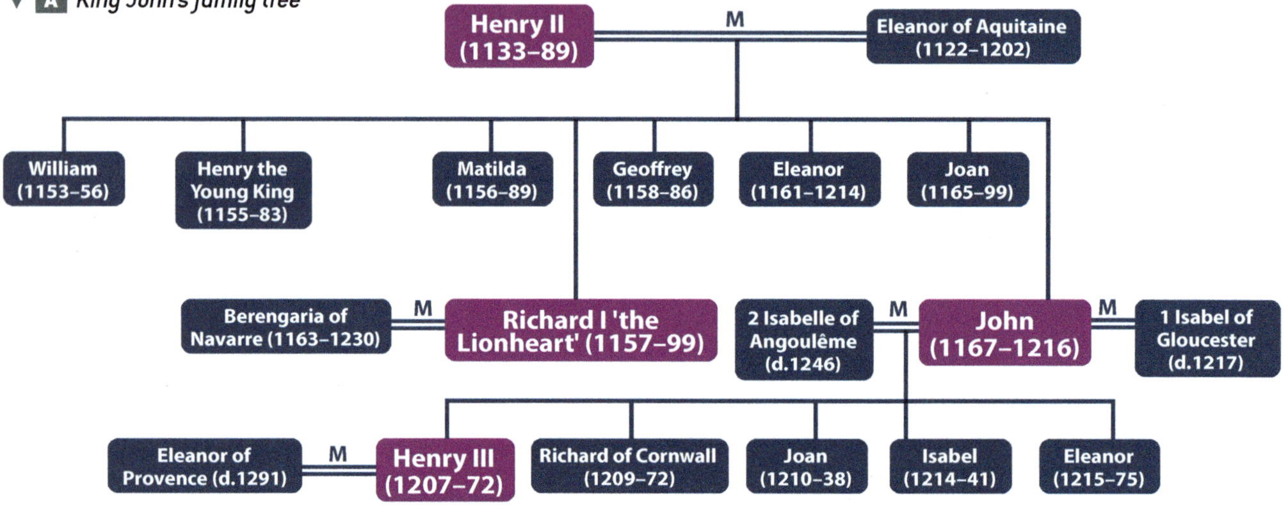

Medieval society

Medieval society was built on the **feudal system**. The king was at the top of this system and gave the barons land, in return for money and men to fight in wars. The barons would then give some of their land to the **knights** if they promised to fight when needed. There was a Great Council where the barons could meet and have their views and concerns heard. However, Medieval kings did not always listen to the Great Council.

'Bad' King John

The Christian religion was an important part of Medieval life. Medieval kings believed they were appointed by God, but the Pope was also the head of the Church and had great power over many European countries. John had a disagreement with the Pope when he refused to support the appointment of Stephen Langton as Archbishop of Canterbury. The Archbishop of Canterbury often found himself as a key adviser to the king; thus, it was a very powerful role. John was against Langton's appointment because he did not want someone who would obey the Pope and go against the king's wishes. In retaliation, the Pope banned church services in England; even marriages and funerals. This frightened the people as they thought that without regular attendance at **mass** they would go to hell. The barons were nervous, as this breakdown in relations between king and Church could lead to an invasion from a foreign king.

▼ SOURCE B *A painting of King John, painted between 1250 and 1259 by Matthew Paris, a monk who did not think highly of John; most images from the time show the king holding a church, trying to show that the king and the Church worked well together*

Another cause of poor relations was high taxes – known as **scutage** – which John charged barons to help him fight wars in France. The barons became angry because John was not living up to their expectations: he was given the nicknames 'lackland' and 'softsword' due to his poor record in battles. This affected the barons as it meant they lost their lands in France, so they lost money. Despite this loss, John continued to charge them even higher feudal payments. To make matters worse John managed to lose the crown jewels in an area of marshland called the Wash! Although this didn't affect the barons as much as raising taxes, it did make people question his competence.

According to the barons and to church officials, John was not doing well as a king, and the barons started to become restless. Few people could read or write in the Middle Ages, so it was down to the educated monks and barons to record the events of the day. As a result, there are many negative historical accounts of John and what kind of king he was, mainly because he came into conflict with the very people who could write down their opinions!

'Good' King John

There was much evidence that John was a terrible king. However, some historians have argued that to be fair, John would never have been able to live up to his father's and brother's great reputations: he would always look inferior. Richard had left John in debt because of his wars with France, so John struggled to raise enough money to govern and defend the country. John himself did win some wars against the Scottish and the Welsh, and strengthened the English navy.

John also ensured that the people of England could have a fair trial with a judge and jury: he sometimes even delayed proceedings so he could be there himself to ensure a trial was fair. This helped everyone in England, not just the rich barons.

Key Words

crusade baron feudal system knight mass scutage occupy

John and the barons

Fed up with John, the barons put an army together under the leadership of Robert Fitzwalter, and sent it to **occupy** London: the barons were ready to fight the king. If John wanted to gather an army of his own, he would need the barons' support. He therefore had no choice but to negotiate with them. On 15 June 1215, King John met the barons at Runnymede, near Windsor. They would negotiate the way in which the country should be governed.

Work

1 a Draw a mind-map of the ideal qualities a Medieval king should have.
  b Annotate your mind-map with comments to explain the ways John did or did not live up to these expectations.
2 Explain why the barons were angry with John.
3 Study **Source B**.
  a How did Matthew Paris portray King John and his relationship with the Church? Think how he has drawn the church and John's crown.
  b Why would he present John in this way?
  c Is this a good source for explaining what kind of king John was? Why or why not?

Fact

To determine whether a source is 'good' or not you should think about the information it gives you and if this is accurate. Then think about what information is missing from the source. Does that make it a 'bad' source? Why has the information been left out?

1.2 What was Magna Carta?

In 1214, the English barons lost patience with their king and raised an army. England was now effectively in a state of **civil war**. It was not uncommon for Medieval kings to face attacks from the barons but this time it was different. The barons would force the king to agree to conditions about how the country was run. John had no option but to agree. Magna Carta was signed on 15 June 1215. What did it mean for John? Would all kings have to agree to it?

Objectives

- **Identify** key features of Magna Carta.
- **Explain** why Magna Carta was significant.
- **Analyse** the significance of Magna Carta.

How did the barons deal with John?

One of the main reasons the barons were angry with John was because of his taxation policy. The most hated tax was scutage. Barons had to pay this if they did not fight for John when he asked. The problem was that the more the barons disliked John, the less likely they were to fight – so the higher the scutage they would have to pay. But there were other reasons why the barons were unhappy; for example, John lost important land in France and fell out with the Pope many times.

On several occasions, the barons drew up a list of complaints about the way John ruled, but he refused to change. Now he had no choice: the barons were prepared to fight him. They had the upper hand and John needed their support to keep power. At Runnymede, the barons got John to sign Magna Carta; Latin for Great Charter. But could the barons trust John?

▼ **INTERPRETATION A** *A print of an engraving by Edmund Evans in 1864, showing King John signing Magna Carta*

Clauses of Magna Carta

Magna Carta contained 63 promises that the barons wanted John to keep. These would change the power of the king and give the barons more control.

▼ **B** *The six main clauses of Magna Carta*

We grant to all **freemen** all the liberties written below:

- a baron's heir shall **inherit** his lands on payment of £100 to the king
- no scutage shall be imposed on the barons except with the common counsel of the realm
- no freemen shall be arrested or imprisoned without a proper trial and according to the law of the land
- the English Church shall be free to make its own appointments
- all **merchants** shall have safety, in staying and travelling in England, for buying and selling goods, free from evil tolls
- a group of 25 barons will be created to monitor the king and ensure he commits to Magna Carta (Clause 61).

John had no intention of sticking to the promises he made that day at Runnymede. He only agreed so the civil war would end, and so he could get the barons back on side. Many people consider it a failure in the short term, because John quickly backed out of the agreement, saying he had been forced to sign it.

◀ SOURCE C *Part of the original Magna Carta*

Key Words

civil war freeman inherit
merchant peasant villein

Extension

The Republic of India also has a plaque at Runnymede that reads: 'As a tribute to the historic Magna Carta, a source of inspiration throughout the world, and as an affirmation of the values of Freedom, Democracy and the Rule of Law which the People of India cherish and have enshrined in their Constitution.'

Research why Magna Carta would be important to the people of India. Does it have the same relevance it has in America?

Why is Magna Carta significant?

It is widely accepted by historians that Magna Carta was not important to all the people of England at the time it was signed. It only referred to freemen, such as barons; **peasants** and **villeins** were not free. The barons were looking out for their own interests when they drew up Magna Carta, and only included the Church and merchants because they needed to get more support against John. Magna Carta changed nothing for the ordinary people of Medieval England, only the politically powerful.

However, as the years passed, Magna Carta developed a greater significance. It applied to more people as they gained their freedom. It introduced the idea that there are some laws and rules that even kings have to follow: kings cannot just do whatever they want. After King John died, other kings signed similar versions of Magna Carta and today it is viewed as one of the first major steps in Britain's journey to becoming one of the world's best-known democracies.

▼ SOURCE D *The American Bar Association (of lawyers) erected this monument at the site where Magna Carta was signed. Although the charter did not change anything for ordinary people at the time, it would become known as a symbol of 'freedom under law'. It was used by the Americans to draw up their constitution when they became independent from Britain in 1776.*

Work

1 Discuss in your group which clauses of Magna Carta you think are the most important. Decide on your top three clauses.

2 Write a paragraph explaining which clause you think would be most likely to make the barons happy.

3 Make a table in your book showing the impact of Magna Carta. One column should be headed 'short-term impacts' and the other should be headed 'long-term impacts'.

Practice Question

Explain the significance of Magna Carta.

8 marks

Study Tip

Remember that something is significant if it was important at the time *and* is also important today. Research the extension task to further develop your response.

1.3 The impact of Magna Carta

King John quickly went back on his word. He had used the signing of Magna Carta as a stalling tactic to allow him to gather troops and rally support. In August 1215, the Pope came out in support of John stating that, as he had been forced to sign Magna Carta, it was invalid. John had the support of the Pope but the barons had the support of the French, whose king was ready to fight John. By May 1216, it looked like a war was about to begin. Would John keep the throne? Would he finally accept Magna Carta?

Objectives

- **Describe** the ways in which King John restored royal control.
- **Explain** the causes and consequences of the Barons' War.
- **Assess** the impact of Magna Carta.

The Siege of Rochester – softsword no more

War had been declared. The barons had taken control of London and had requested support from France, so the French king sent some knights to help secure London. John was in Dover organising his army. Rochester Castle, which lies between the two cities, became vitally important for both King John and the barons.

In a bid to gain an advantage, the barons occupied Rochester Castle. In October 1215, John's men arrived with five **siege** engines, consisting of **catapults** and **trebuchets**. They bombarded the castle with stone balls but they were not strong enough to break through the 3.6-metre-wide stone walls of the castle.

John then waited. He tried to starve the barons out. On 25 November he sent an order to Canterbury to have pickaxes made: he was going to dig beneath the castle. He sent out another order for 40 fat pigs to be brought to him. By the end of November, the king's men had dug a tunnel under the castle's stone foundations. The tunnel's ceiling was supported by wooden props.

▼ **B** *A map of the south of England and northern France, showing London, Dover, Runnymeade and Rochester*

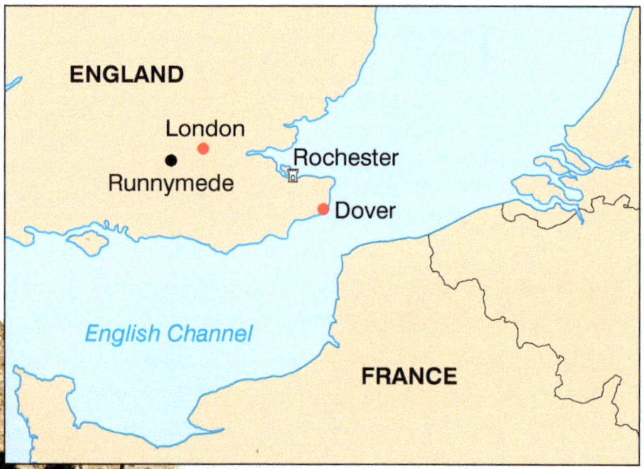

▼ **SOURCE A**
Rochester Castle today; after the 1215 siege it was rebuilt during the reigns of Henry III and Edward I

When the pigs eventually arrived, they were slaughtered and their fat was used to cover sticks that were packed under the wooden props. These were set on fire. The fat burned at such a high heat that the wooden props holding up the castle's wall burned away – and the wall collapsed. John and his men stormed the castle. The siege was over by 30 November. John now held the power, but for how long?

The Barons' War and the re-signing of Magna Carta

Everything seemed to be going John's way. Small rebellions in Scotland and Wales had been settled after his cunning victory at Rochester. John now had control of most of England, as far north as Berwick-upon-Tweed.

However, John felt his fortune change in May 1216. While in Kent, he saw the French Prince Louis arrive with troops. The barons had called for him and promised him the English throne. John fled to southwest England. Louis, with the support of the barons, managed to take control of most of England. He did this by capturing strategic towns and castles. John took land from the rebel barons and gave it to his supporters in a bid to regain control. The barons would not be put off. With the support of a foreign power they could still defeat John: his royal authority had been diminished.

Prince Louis was announced (but not crowned) king at St Paul's Cathedral on 2 June 1216. Even the Scottish King Alexander II swore allegiance to Louis. It seemed like John had lost power and the barons had won.

We cannot be sure that John failed in his last attempt for control as, in October 1216, King John died. The barons decided that they did not need a French king and they crowned John's young son, Henry, instead. This worked in the interest of the barons as Henry, being a child, was easy to deal with. His **regent**, the Earl of Pembroke, called for Englishmen to defend the country against Louis. So, on 28 October 1216, Henry III became king. The barons reissued Magna Carta and the young king agreed to the conditions. Power had been restored and the king had to follow the rules set out. The events of the Barons' War had made it clear what would happen if he didn't.

▼ **INTERPRETATION C** ***From the official Magna Carta 800th anniversary website, 2015. There were many events to mark the anniversary, with a ceremony held at Runnymede attended by the Archbishop of Canterbury, Queen Elizabeth and Prime Minister David Cameron:***

> It has transcended barriers of language and the divisions of cultures and ideologies. 800 years on, the rule of law, individual freedom and human rights are foundational principles of modern societies.

Key Words

siege catapult trebuchet regent parliament

Was Magna Carta a failure?

It is safe to say that the power of the monarch was limited after the signing of Magna Carta. However, the king could simply go against it if he wished. This was a feature of the reign of John's son, Henry III. It was not until 1295, during the reign of Edward I, that there was a **parliament** that represented people other than the barons.

Some historians argue that Magna Carta was a base for the freedom and justice mentioned in Interpretation C to grow. Others argue it was merely a negotiation between John and the barons, not the basis for human rights as we know them today. It is fair to say that although Magna Carta was important to the barons at the time, it was only in the long term, when its full impact could be evaluated, that its significance was clear.

Work

1. Draw a timeline of the events from the signing of Magna Carta to the end of the Siege of Rochester.
2. a. Create a table showing the ways Magna Carta was a success and the ways it was a failure.
   b. Use two different colours and mark which points are short-term and which are long-term successes and failures.
   c. Do you think Magna Carta was a success or a failure at the time? Discuss this with your partner.
3. How did the barons try to protest against King John? Explain your answer.
4. In groups, research Magna Carta and its legacy. Create a presentation evaluating the impact of Magna Carta and whether it has been a success. You should look at the commemorations, human rights law and the impact at the time.

2.1 Simon de Montfort and King Henry III

Magna Carta was a series of written promises between the king and his subjects stating that the king would govern the country with respect for the law. The barons were given the responsibility of making sure the king carried out these promises, and the document clearly stated that they could use force if they felt it was necessary. So Magna Carta put the barons in a much more powerful position: surely there was now nothing that could upset the barons and cause more unrest. Wrong! In 1216, King John died and his son became King Henry III, at only nine years old. Over the next few years, the country was run by a series of advisers, including the king's mother. Henry personally took over in 1234, and before long, his relationship with the barons was at breaking point. There was one baron in particular who came to the fore at this time – Simon de Montfort. Who was de Montfort and what was his relationship with Henry like?

Objectives

- **Summarise** the role of Simon de Montfort in Henry III's court.
- **Explore** the problems between Henry III and the barons.
- **Evaluate** the actions of Henry III in dealing with de Montfort and the barons.

Who was Simon de Montfort?

After the Norman invasion of 1066, the de Montfort family was one of the first **aristocratic** families to come to England from Normandy. However, over the next 200 years they had lost more and more of their land to the king. In 1229, Simon, the leading member of the de Montfort family, tried to reclaim some of the family land, so he approached Henry.

Henry agreed to give the family some land back. Even better, Henry made de Montfort one of his favourites, and gave him the job of **steward**. De Montfort enjoyed this role as it put him in a position to meet rich widows: marrying one might be a way to sort out the family finances. He eventually married Henry's sister, Eleanor. She had been married before, at the age of nine, and was a widow by the time she was 16. De Montfort was then given special favour and sent to represent the king abroad. This position helped him in what was arguably now his main aim – reclaiming land that he felt his wife was owed by her first husband's family. For de Montfort, marrying the king's sister opened up the door to wealth and opportunity.

De Montfort eventually became an opponent of the king and a controversial figure. Some people view him as a hero and the creator of modern **democracy**. Others view him as an opportunistic baron, who got lucky marrying the king's sister.

Key Biography

Simon de Montfort (1208–65)

- The Earl of Leicester from 1239 until his death, de Montfort worked for the king but eventually led a rebellion against him, which resulted in the Second Barons' War.
- He became ruler of England for a short time when the king was imprisoned. He became famous for calling two parliaments. Some people believe these parliaments were the model for our parliaments today; others disagree.
- He died in the Battle of Evesham, August 1265, fighting against the king.

Henry and the Pope

Henry was a **pious** king. Although this was normally seen as a good thing, his links with Rome created financial problems for England. Henry had increased payments to Pope Innocent IV to help the Pope fight wars in Europe. The Pope had convinced Henry to help him remove the royal family of Sicily and put his young son, Edmund, on the throne instead. Four years later, when Henry failed to pay the promised money, another Pope (Alexander IV) threatened to **excommunicate** Henry – remember how the people of England reacted when this happened to John. Furthermore, the Pope suggested that

Henry's brother, Richard, become Holy Roman Emperor: an important job that would bring part of Europe under the control of the Pope. This was a clever move by the Pope as it meant Henry and England would foot the bill for the Sicilian war. This would also mean an increase in taxes for the barons.

Henry then gave away top jobs in English churches to Italian clergy. This stopped English men being promoted in the Church. This led to the barons becoming increasingly frustrated by Henry's subservience to the Pope.

Henry and France

Henry had close ties with the French, especially the House of Lusignan, due to his marriage. This relationship alarmed the barons, as the English severely disliked the French. Their alarm increased when Henry started to allow French men into parliament. This was also down to his tutor and adviser, Peter de Roches: a French man. The barons started to feel that England was coming under foreign rule.

The Gascon campaigns

SOURCE A

A painting of Henry III at his coronation, showing him holding a church and having the crown placed on his head

Henry raised taxes to fund his campaigns to win back the land his father had lost in France. In 1230, he took his army to Brittany and Gascony. He lost the campaign and returned to England. In 1248, Simon de Montfort was sent over to France to try again. He had been training to go on crusade so was ready to fight. He crushed the rebellions and established order with a combination of military skill and ruthlessness. The previously lost land was now under the control of Henry and de Montfort.

The king was happy until reports reached him about de Montfort's use of force against the French in the occupied towns. The king was sympathetic to the French, so he called de Montfort back to England for an inquiry. Despite being found innocent, de Montfort was furious with the king. This anger intensified when Henry insisted his son, Edward, should take charge of the campaign when de Montfort returned to France. De Montfort felt so let down by the king he considered fighting with the French, against the king! He returned to England at the request of the barons, feeling betrayed by the king and bitter at his perceived fall from grace.

Key Words

aristocratic steward democracy pious excommunicate

Henry needs the barons

By 1254, the relationship between the king and the barons had deteriorated. Henry's various schemes, involving land lost in France or more money to the Pope in Rome for wars against Sicily, angered the barons. De Montfort was fast becoming their spokesperson. They refused to fund Henry's schemes. Henry now faced a crisis on two fronts. He needed the support of the barons but they did not support increased taxes. This meant that Henry could not provide the funds the Pope desired. Without the money from increased taxes it was likely he would be excommunicated. Would the barons help him?

Extension

GCSE

Research a biography of Henry III's son, Edward I. Did he learn from observing his father's struggle with de Montfort?

Work

1 Using the biography of Simon de Montfort and the information given, create a CV for him to present to Henry. It should have information about: his personality; his strengths; the reasons why he would a good person to work for the king; his bad points; whether his bad points might make him a bad person to work for the king.

2 Working in groups, write the main problems between the king and the barons on cards. Order these in a 'diamond nine' to show which problems could be the most important.

3 Write a letter to King Henry advising him on his actions towards the barons. What should he have done differently? What did he do well? Can you predict future issues he should try to deal with?

4 Study **Source A**. What impression does this give you of Henry? Think back to the similar portrait of King John.

2.2 The Provisions of Oxford and the Second Barons' War

By 1254, the relationship between the king and his barons was bad. The barons refused to fund Henry's schemes, so he faced a crisis on two fronts. He would either be excommunicated by the Pope for not paying the money he owed, or he would have to get the support of the barons. So he asked the barons for help: they refused. There was a meeting of the Great Council in 1258 and it was here that the barons set out to change the shape of royal control in England. What would this mean for the balance of power?

Objectives

- **List** the changes to power made by Simon de Montfort.
- **Explain** the significance of the Battle of Lewes.
- **Compare** the First and Second Barons' Wars.

The Provisions of Oxford, 1258

Simon de Montfort led the barons who called the Great Council against Henry in 1258. Having previously secured his position of wealth, he became obsessed by the reform of royal control and influence. During the Great Council meeting, the king agreed to the Provisions of Oxford. This stated that from now on a council of 15 barons would be in charge of the Great Council. They would be elected by 24 men: 12 appointed by the king and 12 by the barons. By agreeing to the provisions the king agreed, among other things, that:

- foreign members of the royal household would be banished
- castles would be held by Englishmen
- each county would have a sheriff and taxes would be decided locally.

This settled some of the grievances the barons had about foreign control of England. The barons also refused to fund the planned payment to the Pope over the wars in Sicily.

The Provisions of Oxford gave the barons the majority of power, as they stated that the barons could make decisions without the king's presence or approval. Moreover, the king could not make decisions without approval of the council. The Provisions of Oxford had a real impact on royal authority.

▼ **SOURCE A** *From a section of the Provisions of Oxford, 1258, outlining the powers of the* ***chancellor*** *– the person responsible for the creation of official documents and laws:*

> The chancellor of England will not seal any writ without the order of the king and of the councillors who are present.

Opposition to the Provisions of Oxford

However, some barons were angered by the Provisions of Oxford, especially Richard de Clare, the Earl of Gloucester. He and many other older barons felt that the reforms were interfering with their local interests. The younger barons also disliked the Provisions of Oxford because they had not been elected to the council, and had therefore lost their influence. Furthermore, those lower in society were given a greater say. The barons longed for the feudal system when knights and **burgesses** had much less influence!

The Provisions of Oxford were extended in October 1259, with the creation of the Provisions of Westminster. These provisions reformed local government and were popular among the less powerful and wealthy members of society. Many barons resented the provisions, as they forced them to accept reforms demanded by their **tenants**.

▼ **SOURCE B** *Henry III being forced by his barons to implement the Provisions of Oxford*

Therefore the barons had another reason not to be happy with the settlement de Montfort had agreed to. The barons were clearly divided.

▼ **INTERPRETATION C** *From the website of the British parliament, which provides information about the work of parliament and Members of Parliament. It ran a campaign in 2015 to celebrate the 750th anniversary of Simon de Montfort's challenge to Henry:*

> These reforms show the growing power of social groups beyond the major barons, who though still leading the reform, evidently felt they could not ignore popular discontent. In this regard they introduced reforms that were even harmful to their own local interests.

Henry's return to power

The bickering barons led the way for Henry to return to power and reject the Provisions of Oxford and Westminster. Henry wrote to the Pope and asked for his permission to cancel the provisions. In 1261, Henry received confirmation from the Pope that he would be released from the provisions. He appointed his own men to the council. Henry was back in power and de Montfort left for France in disgust.

Why is the Battle of Lewes significant?

After three years of Henry's revived rule, the barons sent for de Montfort: they had had enough. De Montfort returned and started the Second Barons' War. England was now in the midst of another civil war. The barons were fed up with negotiating and were now using military strength instead. As a result, de Montfort and his men were victorious at the Battle of Lewes in 1264. De Montfort captured the king and imprisoned his son, the young Prince Edward. England was now without its king, and in charge was the opportunistic baron, de Montfort. England was on its way to being a **republic**.

Extension

GCSE

The Simon de Montfort Society run tours along key sites that involved de Montfort. They are considering starting a tour on the site of the Battle of Lewes. They want you to write the script for the tour guide. People need to know why it is significant but they also need to be entertained. You should think about the language you use: try to build a narrative. This means you can give your opinion and you can add in interesting facts about the battle.

Key Words

chancellor burgess tenant republic

▼ **SOURCE D** *A stained glass window at Chartres Cathedral in France showing Simon de Montfort on horseback*

Work

1 a Make a timeline of the key events between 1259 and 1264.
  b Above each event note its cause, and below each event note its consequence.
  c Colour code the causes and consequences into long-term ones and short-term ones.

2 What can we learn from **Source A** about the power of the king under the Provisions of Oxford?

Practice Question

Explain two ways in which the First Barons' War and the Second Barons' War were similar.

8 marks

Study Tip

When dealing with similarity questions you should try to think of different aspects. For example; causes, key features and consequences/outcomes. These will show similarities and you can then explain in more detail using specific evidence.

2.3 The king and a new parliament

King Henry was captured and young Prince Edward was being held in prison. Simon de Montfort had become the most powerful man in England. England was set to become a republic, ruled by a parliament and not a monarch. However, Edward made sure his father regained full control and de Montfort's life ended with him being cut into pieces. Would kings now continue to overrule the demands of the barons? Would the next council come from war or from more peaceful methods?

Objectives

- **Describe** the key features of the barons' challenge to power.
- **Categorise** the consequences of the changes to royal authority.
- **Analyse** the significance of Simon de Montfort.

The Commons: the road to parliament

When Simon de Montfort ruled over England, some barons began to get worried that he was too powerful. Not all the barons supported the new system of the Great Council, as de Montfort had appointed a council of nine which consisted of his own friends and allies; he reconfirmed Magna Carta and the Provisions of Oxford. The barons who had supported Henry wanted their old lives of influence and money back.

In 1265, de Montfort started to worry that he was losing his grip on the country and so he called a meeting of the Great Council. Unlike previous meetings, he invited burgesses and knights from every county. This increased support for de Montfort, which he was lacking from the powerful barons. The burgesses represented the growing merchant class who were making money in the growing towns all over England. So ordinary people – sometimes known as commoners – had been invited to the Great Council to have their voices heard for the first time, in what became known as the Commons. This was indeed a historic event.

The Battle of Evesham, 1265

The barons were concerned with their own interests and were also beginning to think that de Montfort was ruling as an **autocrat**. They began to put all their support behind Henry. His son, Prince Edward, had been released and had raised an army: they were out to get de Montfort.

Later, on 4 August 1265 at the Battle of Evesham, de Montfort fell from his horse, crying 'God's grace!' before he landed. His body was then cut into pieces – even his genitals were cut off – and the pieces were sent around the country as a warning.

▼ **SOURCE A** *An undated painting of de Montfort's death at the Battle of Evesham*

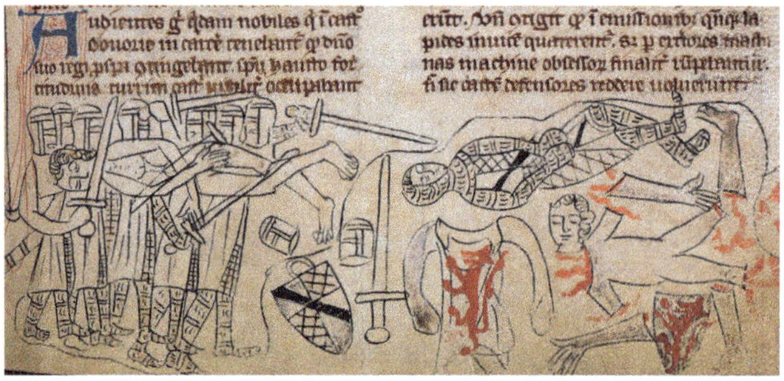

Fact

When de Montfort was killed, his head was cut off and his testicles were hung over his nose. This was sent to Roger Mortimer's wife, who was a big critic of de Montfort. She apparently had a party on receipt of the 'present' and put it pride of place on a lance in the great hall of Wigmore Castle.

Edward and future parliaments

Henry ruled until 1272 and never called another meeting of the Great Council. However, when Prince Edward became King Edward I, he knew he would have to tread carefully with the barons. He had learned from his father's and grandfather's mistakes.

When Edward needed money to fight the Scots and the Welsh to secure his territory and authority, he knew what would happen if he simply demanded the money from the barons, instead of negotiating with them. Therefore, he called many parliaments to raise the funds required. In 1295, he called what would be known as the **Model Parliament**. This is the parliament that most

Key Words

autocrat Model Parliament

▼ **SOURCE B** *A painting of Edward I and his Model Parliament, from the 1300s; notice that some people are smaller than others – a reminder that this is not a completely equal parliament*

resembles ours today. The lords were invited to attend but the commoners (by far the largest group) were elected. This was still not a perfect system as only the elite of society, such as the barons, could vote, and voting was not done in secret.

Does de Montfort deserve to be remembered 750 years on?

De Montfort's parliament was not perfect, and parliament and its powers would continue to change throughout the Middle Ages. The king's power was not totally challenged until the Glorious Revolution, when parliament gained more control than the monarch in 1688. Regardless, what most people agree is that de Montfort was influential in the common man's growth of power; however, women had to wait a few hundred years more for their voices to be heard.

▼ **INTERPRETATION C** *Adapted from* A History of England, *written in 1830 by Sir James Macintosh; he was a supporter of the French Revolution that saw the removal of the French king and royal family:*

> De Montfort summoned a parliament of which the lower house was composed, as it has ever since been, formed of knights of the shires and members for cities and boroughs. He thus unknowingly determined that England was to be a free country.

▼ **INTERPRETATION D** *Adapted from* Simon de Montfort, *written by J. R. Maddicott in 1994; this gives a more balanced account of de Montfort and his parliament:*

> It was the most fundamental attempt to redistribute power within the English state before the seventeenth century. The 1265 parliament was a partisan [biased] assembly in which ecclesiastics [priests] were much over-represented and earls and magnates under-represented.

Work

1. Why did the barons turn against de Montfort?
2. How was the 1295 parliament different from the 1265 one?
3. There are many different consequences to events. Can you explain the political, economic and social effects of the changes between 1265 and 1295?
4. Complete a table with one column for reasons de Montfort should be remembered and another column for reasons he shouldn't.

Practice Question

Explain the significance of Simon de Montfort for the development of democratic government.

8 marks

Study Tip

Something doesn't have to be good to be significant. Split your points into long- and short-term significance. Is there a difference between why de Montfort is significant in 1295 compared to today?

3.1 Were rats to blame for the Peasants' Revolt?

Life for the peasants of England was hard. They were at the bottom of the feudal system, working for a lord and serving the king. In the fourteenth century the peasants decided they had had enough. Not only were they having to pay high taxes to fund the king's lifestyle, but they were also being killed off by a terrible plague that seemed to affect them more than the barons. The peasants fought back against a king and a system that treated them unfairly. What were the main causes of this revolt?

Objectives

- **Outline** the impact of the Black Death.
- **Categorise** the causes of the Peasants' Revolt.
- **Analyse** causes to make a judgement on the most important.

The Black Death arrives

▼ **A** *A map showing the spread of the plague through Europe in the 1300s*

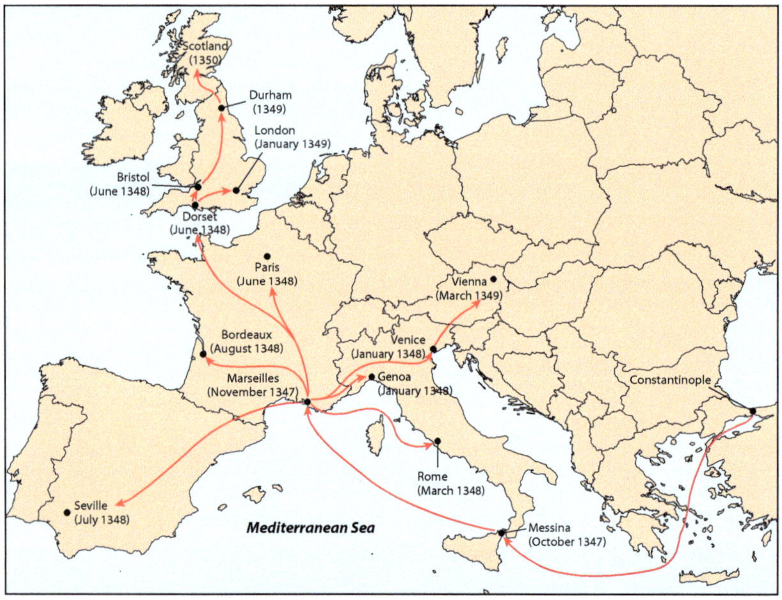

In 1348, a ship arrived at Melcombe Regis in Dorset, bringing goods from Europe. However, also on board the ship was something that quickly swept across England, getting as far as Scotland by 1350, and would eventually go on to kill a third of the population: the plague. The poor were more likely to be affected by the plague. This had a big impact on Medieval society, and became known as the Black Death.

The Statute of Labourers, 1351

The Black Death had the greatest impact on peasants, who made up the majority of the workforce. It led to fields of crops being left to rot, since there weren't enough people to bring in the harvests, and some villages being abandoned. However, for the surviving peasants, there were big advantages.

▼ **B** *Bar graphs showing the decrease in the number of days worked after the Black Death, and the increase in wages paid after the Black Death*

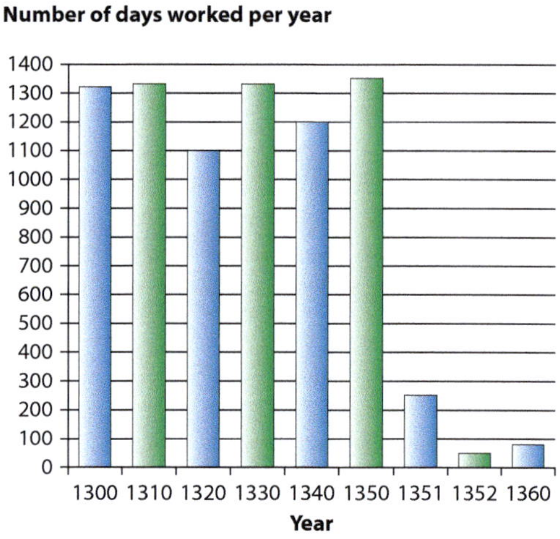

As there were far fewer workers after the Black Death, the peasants started to demand higher wages. Good, strong and hardworking peasants were now in demand. And so to look for better pay, or a fairer lord, many peasants moved to neighbouring villages.

Local lords and even the king started to become worried that the peasants were gaining too much power, and that the feudal system was starting to break down. So, in 1351, Edward III passed the Statute of Labourers.

▼ **SOURCE C** *Adapted from the Statute of Labourers, 1351:*

> Every man and woman in the realm must work for those who want them, and shall only receive the same wages as before the plague.

This angered the peasants. Some who had left their manor (the area their lord owned) were now captured and forced to work for their lord again. However, the peasants didn't just passively accept this new situation. Between 1377 and 1379, 70 per cent of the people brought before the **Justice of the Peace** were accused of breaking the Statute of Labourers. It was clear that the peasants who survived the Black Death were not afraid to stand up for themselves.

Causes of the Peasants' Revolt

The Statute of Labourers tried to control the peasants and their rising wages – but some peasants were in quite a powerful position. After all, the Black Death had killed so many workers, and landowners needed workers to bring in the harvests. The peasants started to question the way the government was running the country. Furthermore, the new king, Richard II, was young and inexperienced. He had taken over from his very able grandfather, Edward III, as his father, Edward the Black Prince, had died the year before. Richard's reputation was not helped by his association with John of Gaunt, his main adviser and one of England's most hated landowners. Gaunt advised Richard to raise taxes.

Richard was also fighting unsuccessful campaigns against the French in the **Hundred Years War**. To help fund these campaigns he introduced a **poll tax**. In fact, he introduced three in as many years! By 1380, every person over the age of 15 had to pay four **groats** per year to the king. This was a massive increase from the one groat they had previously paid.

Furthermore, many priests started to preach about how the Church had been exploiting the peasants. The key people doing this were John Wyclif and John Ball.

Key Words

Justice of the Peace Hundred Years War
poll tax groat pardon

They argued that the Church should not be charging **pardons** for sins and that the Church should not have so much property when others were starving.

In 1381, the peasants had had enough. They started a revolt against the system that they felt suppressed them. The Peasants' Revolt had begun.

▼ **SOURCE D** *Adapted from one of John Ball's speeches, quoted in* The Chronicles of Froissart, *written c1400:*

> My good friends, things cannot go well in England until everyone is equal. They are dressed in velvet while we are forced to wear rags.

Fact

Historians sometimes add a 'c' before dates. This stands for 'circa', which means 'around' or 'approximately'.

Work

1. How did the Black Death arrive in England?
2. Why did the Black Death mean peasants could demand higher wages?
3. Why did King Edward III pass the Statute of Labourers?
4. a Make a list of as many causes of the Peasants' Revolt as you can think of.
   b In groups make colour coded cards of the causes to sort them into factors (political, social, economic and religious).
   c Use the cards to create a mind-map showing the causes of the revolt.
5. Were rats the most important cause of the Peasants' Revolt? Use your own knowledge and the sources to help you. Hint: when thinking about which cause was the most important, try to divide your answer into long- and short-term causes. You could even try to show how these causes link together.

3.2 The Peasants' Revolt of 1381

Life under the Statute of Labourers and an ever-increasing poll tax was hard for ordinary people. To make matters worse, there was a new king in June 1377, Richard II. He was young and inexperienced. Landowners, the Church and the king were taking lots of money from people by raising taxes. Many peasants were returning home from fighting in the Hundred Years War and were being forced back to their old lives – but were now paying far higher taxes. Disgruntled, many peasants refused to pay the poll tax. They threatened violence and decided to march to London, to take their grievances straight to the king. Would he listen?

Objectives

- **Identify** the aims of the Peasants' Revolt.
- **Compare** the actions of both the peasants and the king.
- **Evaluate** the tactics of the peasants.

'When Adam delved and Eve span'

The peasants were inspired by the preaching of John Ball who said, 'When Adam delved and Eve span, who was then a gentleman?' This reference to the creation of man and woman outlined in the Bible shows that there was no rich and poor, thus everyone was equal. The king had Ball arrested so his preaching couldn't influence any more people against the feudal system and the unfair distribution of wealth. The king was clearly worried.

Ball's arrest came too late, however, as the peasants had had enough. Uprisings started in Essex and Kent; the men involved in these uprisings eventually joining forces. They were not necessarily angry with the king, but more with the oppressive system they lived under. They were more interested in removing bad priests and evil landowners, as these were the very people who directly exploited them.

The actions of the rebel peasants and the government

▼ **A** *The key areas and events in 1381, as the peasants made their way to London to see the king*

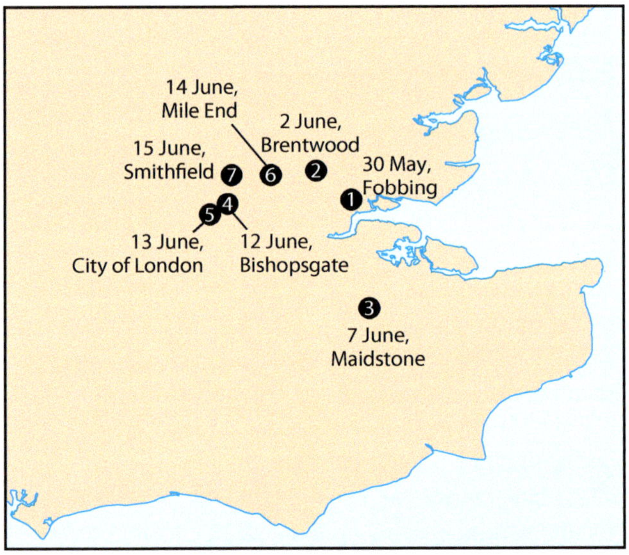

1 30 May, Fobbing

Soldiers turn up to support the tax collector John Bampton who has come to collect the poll tax. The peasants refuse to pay and threaten Bampton with his life. Scared, he rides straight back to London. The villagers hide in the woods as they are worried they will be punished for their actions.

2 2 June, Brentwood

Rebels from other villages join forces. When the Chief Justice is sent to the village to get what Bampton had failed to, the men return and threaten him with death. When the Chief Justice leaves, the men find Bampton's clerks and behead them. They start setting fire to the houses of Bampton's supporters.

3 7 June, Maidstone

Peasants in Kent march to Maidstone. When they get there they hear a man called Wat Tyler speak; the rebels make him their leader. They also free John Ball from Maidstone prison, and storm Rochester Castle. They destroy tax records by burning down government buildings.

4 **12 June, Bishopsgate**

The men make it to the outskirts of London's city walls and set up camp. Leaving the Tower of London, the king sails to meet the peasants. When they see his barge there is so much shouting and booing that the king's men will not let him get off the boat. Convinced they will not breach the city walls, Richard II says he will meet the rebels on 17 June.

5 **13 June, City of London**

The rebels enter the through the city gates, opened by supporters. They storm the Savoy Palace of John of Gaunt and burn it to the ground. They kill foreign merchants and supporters of the king. However, not all the peasants are violent, as Wat Tyler has given explicit orders for the peasants to be peaceful. The king offers to meet the rebels and their leader at Mile End the next day.

6 **14 June, Mile End**

Wat Tyler meets the king and outlines the peasants' demands. The king is to give a royal pardon to all involved and all villeins are to be made freemen. The king agrees and asks the peasants to go home in peace. Some of the peasants go on another killing spree. These men also kill the Archbishop of Canterbury.

7 **15 June, Smithfield**

Richard II meets the rebels again. Tyler is bold and refuses to leave until the king agrees to his demands. He wants a full change to the system of law. He wants Church lands to be given to the people and to get rid of all bishops bar one. The king agrees. However, one of his men steps forward and kills Wat Tyler. The peasants are confused and some are ready to fight. The king rides forward shouting, 'Will you shoot your king? I am your leader, follow me!' The peasants follow the king out of London. The revolt is over.

▼ **SOURCE B** *An illustration from* The Chronicles of Froissart, *written c1400; Froissart was a monk who recorded the events of the revolt. This illustration shows the Archbishop of Canterbury being killed by the rebels.*

Practice Question

How useful is **Source B** to a historian studying the tactics used by the peasants during the revolt?

8 marks

Study Tip

What tactics does the source show you? Does it tell the whole story? You should focus on the content of the source and mine it for all the information you can. Then think about who produced it – can we trust that person?

Work

1. List the aims of the peasants during the revolt.
2. Create and complete a table with one column headed 'Peasants' actions' and the other headed 'King's actions'.
3. **a** Discuss with your partner whether you think the peasants used the correct tactics. Explain your answer.

   b Write a speech for Wat Tyler to deliver to the peasants on 13 June. Use your points from your discussion to help. Will you encourage violence or peaceful tactics?

3.3 The impact of the Peasants' Revolt

It was common for Medieval kings to go back on their word. King John and King Henry both went against the wishes of the people. It seemed to be happening again after the Peasants' Revolt. King Richard had made promises, and the peasants went back to their respective towns and villages. Their leader's head was put on a spike and supporters were hanged from the gallows. Some uprisings took place in other towns but they were easily squashed by local officials. There are many interpretations of the final minutes of the revolt at Smithfield and about the impact of the revolt on society. Did the revolt change anything? How do people view it now?

Objectives

- **Describe** the different interpretations of Wat Tyler's death.
- **Explain** the impact of the Peasants' Revolt.
- **Evaluate** interpretations of the revolt.

The murder of Wat Tyler

When the revolt was over Richard did not keep his promises. He stated, as kings had done before him, that he was forced to make these promises. The rebel leaders were rounded up and hanged. John Ball was hanged and then his body was cut into pieces. His head was stuck on a spike on London Bridge. Next to it was the head of Wat Tyler. There are many different interpretations of the killing of Tyler.

▼ **INTERPRETATION A** *A painting from 1460 showing the death of Wat Tyler; the king is painted twice, once watching the murder of Tyler and again talking to the rebels*

▼ **SOURCE B** *Interpretation from* The Chronicles of Froissart, *written c1400; Froissart recorded the events of the revolt, but wasn't actually there to witness any of it:*

> Tyler still kept up the conversation with the mayor. The mayor replied, 'I will not live a day unless you pay for your insolence.' Upon saying which he drew his sword and struck Tyler such a blow on the head as felled him. As soon as the rebel was down, he was surrounded on all sides so his own men might not see him.

▼ **SOURCE C** *Interpretation written by a monk in York, 1399; again this monk would not have been there, and is creating the account from word of mouth:*

> Tyler dismounted his horse in front of the king, carrying his dagger. He called for some water and then spat it out in front of the king. Tyler then went to strike the king's valet with his dagger. The mayor of London tried to arrest Tyler and because of this Tyler stabbed the mayor with his dagger in the stomach.

▼ INTERPRETATION D *An engraving from around 1840 showing the death of Wat Tyler; this is a dramatic interpretation of his death, portraying Tyler as the victim*

Short- and long-term impact of the revolt

The revolt was not a total failure. The poll tax was never repeated in the Medieval period, although there were similar charges, and taxes were never as high again. Workers' wages began to rise, as the situation from before the revolt was still the same: there was still a lack of workers, so the peasants could demand higher wages. The landowners paid up, as they needed the workers. Also, parliament eventually gave in and stopped trying to control the peasants' wages.

The demands of the rebel peasants were further realised when some were able to buy their own land, because there was so much unused after the Black Death. This freed them from having to work the lord's land. Gradually peasants became independent and within 100 years the peasants were freemen. They had got what they wanted.

What does history say about the revolt?

The Peasants' Revolt is generally considered a significant event in history. It led to change for the peasants and was the first time ordinary people had started a revolt: this had previously been done only by barons and nobles. However, history is written by people with different opinions, which means some people think the revolt is more significant than others. This means we have different interpretations of it.

Key Word

socialist

Some historians believe the revolt was unnecessary. Their interpretations suggest that society was already changing and that serfdom was coming to an end. **Socialist** historians believe the revolt was significant because it was the first working-class rebellion. Some take this further and present the peasants as politicised and organised. This, they believe, marked the beginning of English ideas of freedom.

Extension

GCSE

Research the connection between the Peasants' Revolt, the poll tax, and the Community Charge of 1989/1990–93.

1 a What are the different interpretations of Wat Tyler's death? Include brief quotations to support your answers.
  b Why might there be different interpretations of his death?
  c How does **Interpretation A** show the different views of Wat Tyler's death?
2 Explain the impact of the Peasants' Revolt.
3 Which interpretation of the Peasants' Revolt do you think is the most convincing?

Practice Question

Explain the significance of the Peasants' Revolt for the development of democracy and equality. **8 marks**

Study Tip

Refer to the results of the revolt at the time and how people have thought about it long after the event.

4.1 How did Henry change the Church?

Henry VIII became king in 1509. He is best known for having six wives and being desperate for a son to rule after him. His first wife, Catherine of Aragon, was unable to provide him with a son, so he planned to divorce her and marry Anne Boleyn. But Henry was unable to do so because, as a devout Catholic, he was not allowed to divorce without permission from the Pope. And the Pope would not allow it. However, Henry eventually got his divorce – and managed to change England forever in the process. How did he do it? What exactly did he change, and who did these changes affect?

Objectives

- **Outline** the problems Henry VIII had during his reign.
- **Explain** why the monasteries were useful to Henry.
- **Compare** different reactions to Henry's actions.

England before the Reformation

The Reformation was a religious movement in the 1500s that began as an attempt to reform the Roman Catholic Church. Many people believed that there was a problem with the Church's wealth and its influence in society. Even the king started to question the Church.

The Church had always been an important part of Medieval life. Monasteries were at the centre of many communities, acting as hotels, hospitals and refuges for the poor. Most people were happy with the role of the Church but others started to feel that the monasteries and nunneries were becoming too powerful. It was said that many people inside had forgotten their vows of poverty and were living a life of luxury, while people outside starved. These changing attitudes to the monasteries and the Catholic Church in general were further fuelled by the writings of Martin Luther in 1517.

Key Biography

Martin Luther (1483–1546)

- He became increasingly angry about the clergy selling indulgences for sin: this was when people would give the priests money to get forgiveness for their sins. He believed that Christians were saved through their own faith.
- He translated the Bible into German. His ideas spread throughout Europe and started the Protestant Reformation.

Henry and the Reformation

Henry VIII was a devout Catholic but he was unhappy with the wealth and the power of the Church. Henry saw the Pope as a competing power. People would take direction from the Pope as the head of the Church, but Henry wanted the people of England to listen to him only. He was not a supporter of Luther and the new Protestant religion, but he used these new ideas to go against the Pope and, most importantly, to get a divorce from Catherine of Aragon. The Pope refused to give Henry a divorce, so Henry made himself the head of the Church of England through the Act of Supremacy, 1534. This gave him full control and he no longer had to pay taxes to the Pope in Rome.

Many people refused to recognise Henry as the head of the Church; most famously his Lord Chancellor, Thomas More. Henry had created a law, with the help of Thomas Cromwell, to make it treason not to accept Henry as the head of the Church. Before he was beheaded, More said that he died 'as the king's good servant, but God's first'.

Key Biography

Thomas Cromwell (1485–1540)

- He was a blacksmith's son, and was well travelled.
- He became part of Henry VIII's court, soon becoming his most faithful servant. He helped to secure Henry's divorce and make Henry wealthy again.
- Historians have differing views about him.

▼ **SOURCE A** *Adapted from the Act of Supremacy, 1534:*

> The king, our sovereign lord, and his heirs and successors shall be taken, accepted and reputed the only supreme head on earth of the Church of England.

Dissolution of the monasteries

Henry's divorce was not the only problem he had. Although he had made himself head of the Church of England and had stopped sending taxes to the Pope, he was still spending far too much money. His conflict with the Pope had angered Catholics in other European countries, and he began to worry about invasion by these foreign Catholics. He therefore made sure every change he wanted was made through parliament. This way, he could blame his government for the changes.

Cromwell promised Henry that he would make him the richest king in Europe. One way to do this would be to take the money from the monasteries: these actions became known as the dissolution of the monasteries. The monasteries controlled a quarter of all the land in England and had a combined annual income of £200,000. This was nearly double that of the king. In 1536, parliament passed an act closing all small monasteries that had an annual income of less than £200. Cromwell then set up *Valor Ecclesiasticus*, which was an evaluation of monastery finances. He sent inspectors to the monasteries to see what they were spending their money on. If they were seen not to be run properly they would be closed down and the Crown would take the finances. Reports were sent to Cromwell, and if they were positive they were sent back to be rewritten in a way that showed them in a less positive light.

Responses to the changes

Not everyone was happy with the changes Henry made. The people of England were used to their king increasing taxes. They were used to quarrels with the Pope. They did not, however, support a complete break with Rome, leaving the king in full control.

Why were people unhappy about Henry's changes?

Rising prices
Prices normally stayed the same every year, but they continued to rise under Henry. People blamed his advisers.

Changes to religion
Many people disliked the changes made to the Church. They wanted the monasteries back and the Pope as head of the Church.

Landowners lost influence
Many landowners who had been advisers to the king fell out of favour after the divorce. They had been supporters of Catherine and felt pushed out. They blamed Cromwell.

Cromwell's power
Cromwell was seen as the creator of the new religious policies and he had helped Henry get a divorce from Catherine. Many of the landowners disliked him, as he was the son of a blacksmith and therefore seen as not good enough to advise the king.

Work

1. Why did Henry VIII want to be head of the Church?
2. Why did Henry let Thomas Cromwell make so many decisions?
3. Explain how the monasteries could solve Henry's problems.
4. Create a conversation between a peasant and a landowner. You should explain why the peasant is angry with Henry, and the same for the landowner. Do they agree with each other's points? Are there some points they disagree on?

Practice Question

Was religion the main factor that made Henry VIII want to take control of the English Church?

16 marks

SPaG: 4 marks

Study Tip

You will need to explain your answer with reference to religion and other factors. Consider the economic, political and personal factors. Can you create links between these factors? Does one have more importance than the others?

4.2 The Pilgrimage of Grace

By 1536, King Henry VIII had divorced Catherine of Aragon, married Anne Boleyn (who had a baby on the way), and had taken a firm grip of the Church. He had got what he wanted; he controlled the Church, and had a new wife and possibly a son. He had another surprise waiting for him, though – an uprising. Peasants from Yorkshire started to march towards London. They wanted Henry to listen to their demands and return the Pope as the head of the Church. They also wanted the return of the monasteries. Did Henry return the monasteries to his people? How did the protestors present their demands?

Objectives

- **List** the demands of the pilgrims in 1536.
- **Explain** the causes of the Pilgrimage of Grace.
- **Compare** and contrast the rebellion with the Peasants' Revolt.

Fact

A pilgrimage is a journey of moral or religious importance, normally to a shrine or location of importance. A pilgrim is a person that undertakes a pilgrimage, sometimes to spread their faith.

Demands of the pilgrims

In 1536, a rebellion broke out in Yorkshire. It was an uprising by devout Christians who were worried and angered by the changes that Henry had made to the Church. They had to be careful because the change in law meant that criticism of religious changes was a criticism of the king. They could be charged for treason. They found a leader in a lawyer called Robert Aske. He was able to put the case together for the group to show that they were not against the king. In fact, Aske and his fellow protestors all believed in the social hierarchy and royal authority. They had no intention of challenging Henry. They just wanted him to:

- restore the monasteries (in the north of England the monasteries did important social work and were not as corrupt as some in the south)
- recognise the Pope as the head of the Church
- dismiss Cromwell and other ministers who were giving the king poor advice.

The king and others would be in no doubt of the purpose of this pilgrimage, known as the Pilgrimage of Grace, since the marchers carried a banner showing the five wounds of Christ. This uprising was about religion and was against those who were seen to be corrupting it.

▼ **SOURCE A** *The banner under which the pilgrims marched, showing the five wounds of Christ*

▼ **SOURCE B** *Adapted from a speech by Robert Aske, 1536:*

> The closing of the monasteries means that religious services will not be carried out, and the poor will not be looked after. The monasteries are much loved by the people.

Norfolk marches north

Throughout October 1536, the pilgrims captured key locations. The rebellion began in Lincoln with Lord Hussey, who had been a staunch supporter of Catherine. He, and others, wanted a removal of taxes in peacetime. Then York and Pontefract Castle, which had been held by Lord Darcy, a supporter of Henry, were captured. Darcy surrendered to the pilgrims and joined their campaign. By the end of October they had control of most of England, north of Cheshire and Lincolnshire.

▼ **INTERPRETATION C** *An engraving from 1870 showing marchers taking part in the Pilgrimage of Grace in 1536*

Henry was worried. However, he chose just the right man to represent him and negotiate with the pilgrims: the Duke of Norfolk. Norfolk was a Catholic and a critic of Cromwell. The king was sure he would be the man to deal with the pilgrims. On 27 October he met the pilgrims at Doncaster Bridge; he had an army of 8000 men, and Aske had one of 30,000. Norfolk reassured Aske that he would present a list of demands straight to Henry. The rebels took a month to draw up their demands. They were the same as before except this time they added that a parliament must meet in York. They now wanted better representation for the north.

Norfolk reassured Aske and the rebels that royal pardons would be given. Aske took off his pilgrim's badge and the rebels went home.

Aske and Henry

In December 1536, after the list of demands had been given to the king, Robert Aske spent the Christmas holiday with Henry at his palace in Greenwich.

▼ **SOURCE D** *From a quote by Henry VIII to Robert Aske, December 1536:*

> Be you welcome, my good Aske; it is my wish that here, before my council, you ask what you desire and I will grant it.

▼ **SOURCE E** *From Robert Aske's reply to Henry VIII, December 1536:*

> Sir, your majesty allows yourself to be governed by a tyrant named Cromwell. Everyone knows that if it had not been for him the 7000 poor priests I have in my company would not be ruined wanderers as they are now.

Henry did not disagree with Aske regarding Cromwell. He reassured Aske that he, and the other rebels, had his support. Meanwhile, news was reaching the rebels that the king was strengthening his garrison in the north: he had no intention of sticking to his word. The rebels decided to strike first.

The revolt breaks out again

In January 1537, castles in Hull, Beverley and Scarborough were attacked by the rebels. This gave Henry the excuse he needed to cancel the pardons. Norfolk travelled north again and a further rebellion took him to Carlisle. The rebels surrendered and 74 of them were hanged in their own gardens. Norfolk did not hang more because he felt they had been humiliated enough. The second wave of the rebellion had been squashed.

Work

1. **a** List the aims of the Pilgrimage of Grace.
   b Pick the one you think is the most important. Explain why you picked this one.
2. Why was the Duke of Norfolk the right man to negotiate with the pilgrims?
3. Create a story board showing the causes of the Pilgrimage of Grace. You should think about the different types of causes and explain them with captions.
4. Which factor do you think was the most important for causing the Pilgrimage of Grace?
5. Draw a Venn diagram. One circle is for the Peasants' Revolt and the other is for the Pilgrimage of Grace. The overlap of the circles should show similarities between the rebellions.

Practice Question

Explain two ways in which the Peasant's Revolt and the Pilgrimage of Grace were similar.

8 marks

Study Tip

You should focus on causes, the methods of the rebels, and the king's responses. Plan out your answer so you can structure this carefully.

4.3 Impact of the rebellion

King Henry VIII had been challenged by the Catholic landowners who had lost their influence after his divorce from Catherine. He was challenged by peasants who were worried about the changes he was making to the Church. They wanted their monasteries back. The one uniting factor for these different social groups was their distrust and disdain for one of Henry's advisers – a man named Thomas Cromwell. How did Cromwell deal with the rebels?

Objectives

- **Describe** the end of the Pilgrimage of Grace.
- **Explain** the impact of the rebellion.
- **Analyse** the role Cromwell played in key events.

Thomas Cromwell takes charge

In the aftermath of the Pilgrimage of Grace, Henry called for Aske, Darcy and Hussey. When they arrived in London they were immediately arrested. Cromwell took a harder line than Norfolk: he was adamant that all those who had gone against the king should be killed. Cromwell was keen to remain as Henry's most faithful servant, and he was also annoyed at people getting in the way of his reforms. Aske was killed in York on 12 July 1537. All local landowners were required to come and watch his execution. Darcy and Hussey had been beheaded the previous year in London. Lord Darcy, at his beheading, told Cromwell that the rebellion was his fault and warned him that there may be one noble left in the country that may take his head, like he had taken Darcy's and Hussey's.

The end of the monasteries

Henry's reaction to the Pilgrimage of Grace sealed the fate of the monasteries. The campaign against smaller monasteries in 1536 now gave way to the dissolution of larger monasteries in 1539. Some abbots tried to resist the closures, for example the Abbot of Glastonbury. He was dragged through the town, hanged, and had his head placed on a spike on the abbey gates. The monasteries were coming to an end.

Monastery land was bought by some landowners. Many monasteries were left empty, having been stripped of the gold and jewels by the monks. The doors, beams, lead and stained glass windows were taken by locals. It is thought that many Tudor houses still standing today have monastic beams in them.

▼ **SOURCE A** *Many abbeys, such as Byland Abbey, were left in ruins after Henry's actions*

▼ **SOURCE B** *The* Mary Rose, *one of the first ships to be able to fire a full broadside of cannons; the ship was built in Portsmouth, 1509–10, and is thought to be named after King Henry VIII's sister Mary and the rose, the Tudor emblem*

Henry gets what he wants

Court finances improved greatly after the pilgrimage, with the money from the monasteries. Henry spent this money developing the Royal Navy, building more ships like the *Mary Rose*, and reinforcing fortifications; he was still worried about foreign attack.

In the long term Henry consolidated his control in the north with the Council of the North. He increased the power of loyal families and secured the border with Scotland. In the short term Henry was convinced about the need for the end of the monasteries and was adamant that he should have control over all people and institutions.

No more rebellions took place during Henry's reign. He had dealt with the Pilgrimage of Grace with deceit and ruthlessness. The 200 executions that took place at the end of the uprising were a warning to those who dared to challenge Henry's authority. Even Thomas Cromwell was executed. He had fallen out of favour with the king and was charged with treason and corruption. One of the things Henry blamed Cromwell for was encouraging him to marry Anne of Cleves, his fourth wife, who was not to his liking. Cromwell was beheaded in July 1540: Darcy's prediction had come true. King Henry VIII now had full control of the Church and his country.

▼ **SOURCE C** ***A woodcut showing Henry sitting on his throne with the Pope under his feet, as a foot stool***

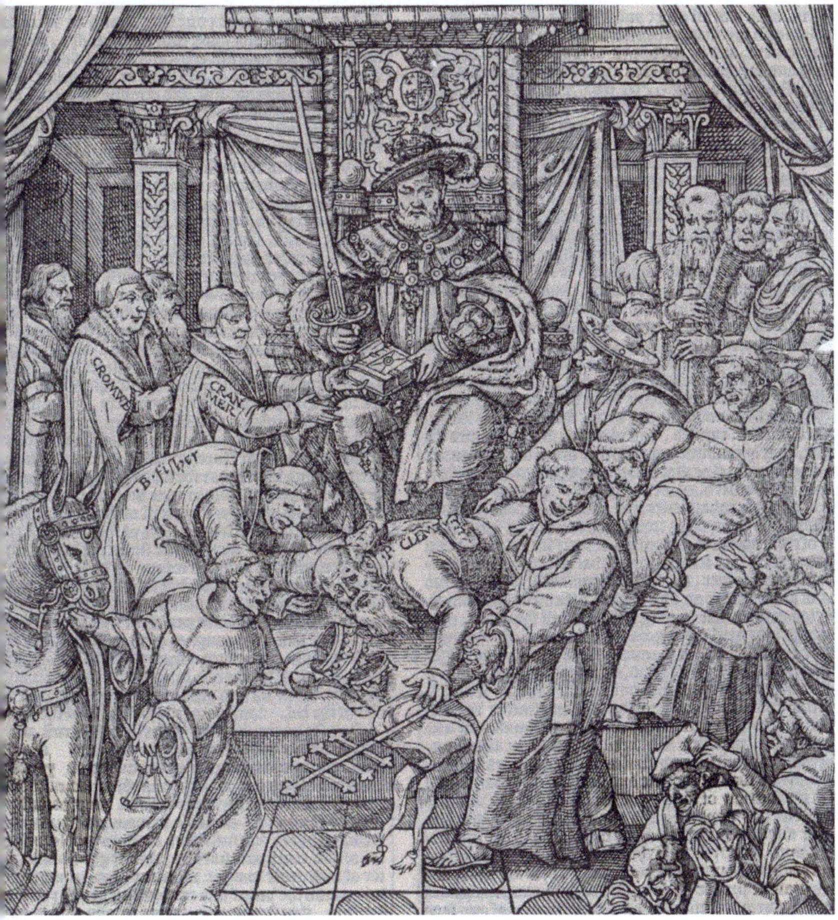

Extension

Wolf Hall, Bring Up the Bodies and *The Mirror and the Light* are novels written by Hilary Mantel that explore the life of Thomas Cromwell. Many historians have criticised Mantel for distorting the truth, and accuse her of trying to rescue Cromwell from his bad reputation. Research this on the Internet to see what historians have said about the novels. Do you think her account stands up to what you know about Cromwell? You should read them and see what you think!

Work

1. a. Describe the end of the Pilgrimage of Grace.
   b. Would you say the pilgrimage was a defeat or a victory for the rebels?
2. a. Explain the impact of the rebellion.
   b. With two different colours, underline the short- and long-term impacts in your answer.
   c. Go back and look at your comparison to the Peasants' Revolt. Do you think they are more similar, now you know the impact the pilgrimage had?
3. a. Study **Source B** and **Source C**. Make notes about what each one shows you about the impact of the Pilgrimage of Grace.
   b. Why were these sources created? Do they have a clear purpose?
   c. Which source do you think is the most useful for a historian studying the impact of the Pilgrimage of Grace? Explain your answer.
4. Henry VIII called Cromwell his 'most faithful servant'. Do you think this was the case when you consider Cromwell's role in controlling the rebellion? Show both sides of the argument.

5.1A The causes of the English Revolution

In the seventeenth century England faced a civil war, with parliament fighting against the king. It involved Scotland and Ireland, and ended with parliament executing the king. This was a British revolution, and there were many reasons why it took place. What were the key causes of the revolution? Was the king ultimately to blame?

Objectives

- **Consider** the differences between King James I and King Charles I.
- **Categorise** the long- and short-term causes of the English Revolution.
- **Analyse** the different causes of the civil war to make a judgement.

James I & VI

When Elizabeth died in 1603, James VI of Scotland became James I of England and, for the first time, Scotland and England shared the same monarch. James was an extravagant king who spent money unwisely, and this led to tension with parliament when they refused to give him any more money or raise it through taxes. They knew James would give the funds to his favourites at court. However, one area that James succeeded at was religion. He managed to keep the majority of Catholics and Protestants content throughout his reign.

Charles I

When Charles I became king in 1625 he was keen to keep order in his court. He believed in the **divine right** of kings and felt that the royal court should be removed from everyday life. He believed he had been appointed by God and did not want many people involved in the decisions about the country. Where his father had been open and had many in his court, Charles closed the doors to allow only a privileged few. He wanted to make decisions that suited him without being challenged. He made the Duke of Buckingham a favourite (he had also been a favourite of James), which alarmed parliament because of the influence Buckingham had over the king. Charles responded by simply dissolving parliament in 1629, and did not call it for another 11 years. Some people refer to this as the period of personal rule but others call it the 'Eleven Years' **Tyranny**'.

▼ **SOURCE A** *Anthony van Dyck's painting of Charles I, painted 1637–38*

▼ **INTERPRETATION B** *Adapted from* A History of England, *written in 1920 by the historian James Oliphant; he writes about Charles's personality:*

> Charles I was a handsome man with cultivated tastes, but he was unfit for the position of king. He was too stupid and cold-hearted to understand or sympathise with the feelings of the people, and events were to prove that he was hopelessly obstinate, self-centred, and untrustworthy.

Foreign policy and the economy

King Charles, like King James before him, had a persistent problem: money. They both needed lots of it from parliament to fight wars, specifically with Spain. James was refused this money as he spent much of it on gifts for his favourites. Charles was refused it because parliament felt they couldn't trust him. There were concerns about the sincerity of his religious tendencies; not helped by his marriage to a Catholic. There was also a fear that he would use the money to become independent from parliament. Charles, who believed it was his divine right to have the money, introduced a tax known as 'Ship Money' in 1637. This was a tax that was normally paid by those in coastal towns as a means of raising money to build the navy. Charles made everyone pay the tax. Parliament was concerned about Ship Money because it could make Charles financially independent and therefore able to make decisions without consulting parliament.

People refused to pay Ship Money. One Member of Parliament, John Hampden, refused and was taken to court. He was narrowly convicted, and the case publicised the opposition towards Charles and his personal rule.

Tensions over religion

After Henry VIII's changes to the Church, England had gradually become more Protestant. However, there were still many Catholics in England – many of them worshipping in secret – and some Protestants regarded them as a threat. After all, there were Catholic plots against Queen Elizabeth, and the famous Gunpowder Plot of 1605 was a Catholic attempt to kill Charles' father, James. Religion was a contentious issue in the seventeenth century.

Charles was not Catholic but he did marry a Catholic princess from France, Henrietta Maria. When Buckingham was killed in 1628, she became Charles' closest adviser. The people of England were scared of her influence and what this could mean for their Church.

The person who went on to have the most influence over religion in England was William Laud. He was made Archbishop of Canterbury in 1633 and felt the same as Charles about bringing conformity back to the Church. Laud was not Catholic, but he was Arminian, which meant he thought people should worship in a similar way to Catholics. For example, he wanted the church clergy to be more separate from the congregation and to be dressed in robes that showed their importance; he also wanted churches to be more decorated, with candles, crosses, statues and paintings.

Laud's changes met so much opposition because many **Puritans** – who were Protestants who wanted the king to reverse the **Laudian** reforms – had become prominent in parliament. They were vocal in their opposition. One famous case of opposition was from three men: Prynne, Bastwick and Burton, who wrote a **pamphlet** criticising the Church. The men were tried in the **Star Chamber**, which had become a substitute for parliament during Charles' personal rule. It was used against anyone who spoke out against the king and Laud, and was known for being corrupt because it always came down on the side of the king. Prynne, Bastwick and Burton were punished as thieves would be: **pilloried**, their faces branded, and their ears cut off.

What Laud and Charles had not expected was the widespread support for the men. When they were released from prison they were met by a large cheering crowd, and when their ears were cut off people crammed to dip their handkerchiefs in the blood. These men were seen as heroes.

Key Words

divine right   tyranny   Puritan   Laudian
pamphlet   Star Chamber   pilloried

▼ **SOURCE C** *A cartoon from c1635, showing the Archbishop of Canterbury, William Laud, choosing a meal made from the ears of Puritans rather than food fit for a prince*

Work

1 a Write three things that you know about James I & VI.
  b Write three things you know about Charles I.
  c Are there any ways in which the kings are different?
2 Explain the grievances that parliament had with King Charles. Try to categorise these into economic, religious and political grievances.
3 a What information does **Source C** give us about the problems people had with Charles?
  b Why was this cartoon created? What was its purpose?

5.1B The causes of the English Revolution

The Scottish rebellion and the Covenanters

Charles' changes in religion also caused unrest in Scotland. The Scots had always had their own Church which by this time was **Presbyterian**, which is a type of Protestantism. However, in 1637, the king insisted that everyone in Scotland should use the new Laudian prayer book. This relied on the **catechism** – religious instruction from the priest – and moved away from the Protestant method of personal worship. There were riots in St Giles' Cathedral in Edinburgh: the Scots would not be told how to worship. In 1638, they signed an agreement called a covenant, saying they would not accept the changes. The people who signed it and its supporters became known as the Covenanters. When Charles sent an army to Scotland in 1639, the Covenanters defeated it. They then invaded England.

▼ **SOURCE D** *Rioting at a church service in St Andrews, Scotland, after the introduction of the Common Prayer Book in 1637. The people can be seen throwing objects.*

The Short Parliament and continued opposition

Charles needed more money if he was going to defeat the Scots. Eleven years after he had dissolved parliament, he needed to ask it to meet again, in April 1640. Parliament agreed to provide Charles with funds to fight the Scots, but only with conditions. He had to promise not to pass laws without parliament's agreement, not to raise unpopular taxes, and to stop Laud's religious changes. This parliament was called the Short Parliament as it lasted only a month. Charles would not give in to parliament's demands.

The Earl of Strafford

One of Charles' favourites was Thomas Wentworth, the Earl of Strafford. He had been sent to Ireland to keep control. There was tension in Ireland between Catholics and Protestants in social and political life. Many of the Protestants were from Scotland and England, and had been originally sent to Ireland by James and Charles to keep order and prevent any rebellions; these postings were known as plantations.

Parliament was not happy about Strafford's control in Ireland. He had a strong and loyal army and parliament was concerned that Charles would try to bring this army to England and use it against the English. When parliament refused to give Charles the funds to fight the Scots, Strafford encouraged Charles to rule England on his own, without parliament.

The Long Parliament

Another parliament was called by Charles in November 1640. Charles was running out of options and was keen to defeat the Scots and restore order. He knew he needed parliament.

▼ **E** *The demands of parliament, November 1640, and what the king had agreed to by the summer of 1641*

Parliament's demands:	The king agreed that:
• Wentworth and Laud must be removed. • Ministers should be appointed from parliament to advise Charles. • The king must get rid of the Star Chamber. • Parliament must meet regularly. • No taxes without parliament's approval. • Reversal of Laudian reforms.	• Strafford was executed and Laud was imprisoned. • Some of Charles' critics were appointed as his advisers. • Courts of the Star Chamber were abolished. • Parliament would meet every three years. • The Long Parliament could be dissolved by Charles without its permission. • Ship Money was made illegal.

Many people were convinced that the agreements would mark an end to the unrest. However, in August 1642 the English Civil War began. What led to this?

Rebellion in Ireland

When Strafford returned to England in 1640, riots broke out in Ireland. Thousands of Protestants were killed by Catholics. Many people in England thought that Charles supported the rebellion: they saw it as a Catholic plot. Parliament was willing to give money to suppress the Irish rebellion but it did not want Charles in charge of the army. Despite Charles' response to parliament of, 'By God! Not for an hour!', parliament took control of the army. The king was furious.

1642 and the Five Members

By 1642, relations had deteriorated again between the king and parliament. John Pym, a leading opponent of the king, presented the Grand Remonstrance This was a list of grievances towards Charles, and was the straw that broke the camel's back. Charles would not be made a fool of by parliament. He raised an army and marched to parliament to arrest the five men – the Five Members – who led the opposition. They had already escaped but now everyone knew how far Charles would go to protect himself. This was even more proof that he was a tyrant who would not listen to the people.

▼ **INTERPRETATION F** *An engraving, from 1803, showing Charles I attempting to arrest the Five Members*

Key Words

Presbyterian catechism

Work

1 a Put the events from 1637 to August 1642 on a timeline.
  b Above the timeline, describe the event; below it, explain why it would cause unrest.
  c Pick the event that you think was the spark for the English Civil War.
2 It has been said that Charles' problem was not England but how he dealt with Scotland. How far do you agree?

Extension

GCSE

Research the lives of each of the Five Members. Who were they and what happened to them – Hampden, Haselrig, Holles, Pym and Strode?

Practice Question

Was religion the main factor in causing the English Civil War?

16 marks

SPaG: 4 marks

Study Tip

You need to explain your answer with reference to religion and other factors. Plan out your answer with all the different events and people you will talk about – see how many link to religion and how many link to other factors. Is there a difference between the short- and long-term factors?

5.2 The English Civil War and the role of the New Model Army

In August 1642, Charles was in Nottingham. He called on his loyal supporters, and declared war on parliament. England was now at war, with itself! The English Civil War had begun. For the next six years parliament and the king fought each other using their loyal forces. Mothers, sons, fathers and daughters fought in a quest to win the war, even if it meant fighting against each other. What were they fighting for? How did they fight the war?

Objectives

- **Define** the different sides of the English Civil War.
- **Explain** the key events of the civil war.
- **Evaluate** the role of the New Model Army in the civil war.

Who fought whom?

The war was fought on two sides: the Roundheads (parliament) against the Cavaliers (royalists). It is generally agreed that people's social class affected who they supported. The wealthy landowners supported the king, as a way to show personal loyalty and to keep in place the social structure they benefited from. The middle classes and peasant workers supported parliament, as there was a less rigid social hierarchy in parliament.

There were also clear geographical allegiances. The king's support was mostly from the north, and parliament had support in the south and in London. This was partially due to a merchant class (traders and business men, for example) who were not happy about the taxes Charles had been imposing.

Religious and political reforms brought in by Charles gave many people good reason to go against him and support parliament. Furthermore, many people simply felt that Charles' personality did not make him a good king.

There were reports that some families divided their loyalties so that no matter who won, they would be on a winning side. Many poorer people were forced to support whoever their lord supported.

▼ **A** *The land held by Charles I and key battles of the English Civil War*

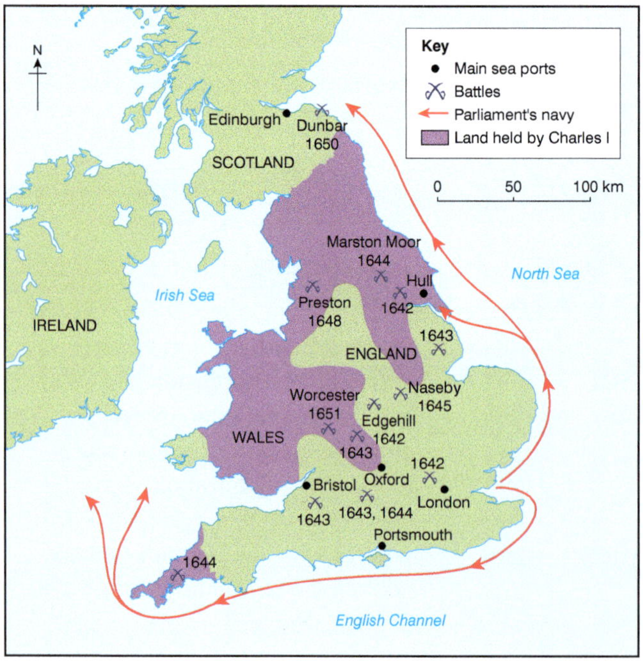

Propaganda as a tactic

The first battle of the war, the Battle of Edgehill in 1642, had no clear winner. The king tried to take London but failed, and withdrew to Oxford. Both sides fought using **cavalry** and **infantry**, and used tactics that had been seen in many battles before.

The king's nephew, Prince Rupert, was one of the most prominent royalist commanders. He led successful campaigns against parliamentary forces and this earned him a bad reputation among the Roundheads.

To combat his successes, parliamentary forces created **propaganda** against Rupert and his trusty dog, Boy, who would accompany him into battle. Propaganda is still used today; it is designed to wear the opponent down and make people turn against them. This worked in the case of Rupert, as it made people think he was weak; it created the idea that the king was weak. Look at the following examples of propaganda and consider why they would have been created.

▼ **SOURCE B** *A Puritan propaganda drawing from 1644 showing royalist forces murdering women and children*

▼ **SOURCE C** *A woodcut showing Prince Rupert hiding in a bean field at the Battle of Marston Moor, 1644, with the dog Boy lying dead in the battlefield*

▼ **SOURCE D** *A drawing showing parliamentary forces smashing up a church*

Key Words

cavalry   infantry   propaganda

The New Model Army and Naseby, 1645

It is important to remember that not all parliamentarians wanted the full removal of the monarchy. They just wanted the removal of royal reforms. This attitude angered Oliver Cromwell. He was the Member of Parliament for Cornwall and had been leading the Roundheads against the Cavaliers, with Thomas Fairfax. Fairfax was a lord who had once worked with Charles to fight the Scots; he joined the parliamentary forces in 1642.

Cromwell was committed to removing the king. He knew that the Battle of Marston Moor could have been a defeat for his side and he did not want that to be the case again. He trained a new army which would be known as the New Model Army. He recruited men based on their ability, rather than their privilege. The army was disciplined and lived by a strict religious and moral code. The men were not allowed to drink or swear.

This army was used for the first time at the Battle of Naseby in 1645. The New Model Army, with 14,000 men, outnumbered the king, with 9000 men. They defeated the royalist cavalry by slowly approaching, rather than charging. They overcame the royalist infantry by manoeuvring behind them and attacking from the rear. Naseby was the end of the king's last great army. The New Model Army, under Cromwell, went on to capture Bristol and then Oxford in 1646. There was now little doubt about who would win the war.

Fact

Women played a big part in fighting the civil war. They mostly worked as nurses but they did defend castles from enemy forces. There are accounts that at Marston Moor, Jane Ingleby of Ripley Castle charged with the royalist forces.

Work

1 Create a profile for each side during the war. You should include details of location, religion and social class.

2 Copy and complete the table below for **Sources B**, **C** and **D**. Which source is the best for finding out about the civil war?

Source	What does it tell us?	Who is winning?	Why was it produced?

3 Could parliament have won the war without the New Model Army? Try to show both sides of the argument.

5.3 Were the English right to kill their king?

The king had tried to restore his control over England and Scotland but Cromwell's New Model Army proved too strong. Charles was captured in 1647 by the Scots in Nottinghamshire, and imprisoned. He would go on trial accused of treason. The king was killed on a cold January day in 1649. Why did parliament feel the only option was **regicide**? Did everyone agree? Who ruled now the king was dead?

Objectives

- **Describe** Charles I's execution.
- **Explore** the reasons why the king was executed.
- **Assess** the evidence to make a judgement about the execution.

Second Civil War

While Charles was imprisoned he was keen to negotiate with parliament to secure a peaceful end to their disagreements. However, at the same time, he was writing to the Scottish parliament to convince them to raise arms against the English parliament and the New Model Army. He promised them a Presbyterian Church in England. The Scots did raise an army against Cromwell and so the Second Civil War began. The two sides met at the Battle of Preston, 1648. The Scots were defeated and Charles had proved he could not be trusted.

The Rump Parliament

In December 1648, the regiment of Colonel Thomas Pride surrounded the Houses of Parliament and refused entry to Members of Parliament who were known to support negotiations with the king. Thomas Pride was a soldier in the civil war and had fought with Cromwell against the Scots. His actions became known as 'Pride's **Purge**', and meant the king would stand trial with no supporters. The remaining members formed a parliament that was known as the Rump Parliament.

The trial of Charles I

Charles was called before parliament where a special commission had been put in place to try him for treason. However, out of the 135 commissioners due to attend, only 68 turned up. They were scared, as they had openly fought against him; this was not the way society worked. Even Thomas Fairfax did not attend. His wife did, and is reported to have supported the king. For many people things had gone too far. However this was not the case for Oliver Cromwell. When Charles walked into court Cromwell said, 'I tell you we will cut his head off with the crown upon it.'

▼ **SOURCE A** *King Charles responded to the charges against him:*

> I would know by what power I am called here. I want to know by what authority, I mean lawful. Remember I am your king, your lawful king.

Another problem parliament encountered was that Charles refused to give a plea – he would not say whether he was guilty or not guilty. He said parliament had no right to act as judge and jury. They could not try the king for treason.

On the second day, the court president, John Bradshaw, allowed the king to speak. They exchanged angry words and Bradshaw ordered the king to be removed. Bradshaw must have known that there was a chance that proceedings would get heated as he wore a specially made bulletproof hat!

With no progress yet made, on 24–27 January witness statements were heard – none in support of Charles. The court heard that Charles:

- was guilty of starting the war by trying to raise an army in Nottingham
- approved of the ill-treatment of parliamentary forces during the war – calling his own subjects enemies
- was plotting with his son to start another war while negotiating with parliament.

On 27 January 1649, parliament found King Charles I guilty of treason and sentenced him to death. Bradshaw justified this by saying that Charles had not done his duty by calling regular parliaments, attacking the basic liberties of the country. Charles would be beheaded.

▼ SOURCE B *An engraving showing the trial of Charles I*

Execution

At 10:00am on 30 January 1649, the king was taken to Whitehall to be executed. Parliament made Charles wait hours. This was partly down to the executioners not turning up – they were too scared to be the one to kill the king – and partly down to **legislation**. Parliament had to secure a law that said no new monarch could be installed on the king's death. The axe fell and the English Revolution was over.

▼ SOURCE C *A painting of the execution of Charles I*

Was Charles a danger to democracy?

People were motivated by many factors to support the execution of the king. There were religious, political and moral objections to the way Charles had been ruling. The soldiers saw Charles' defeat in battle as a sign that God was against him. Other people wanted an end to the taxes they had endured under his reign. The system of taxation was reorganised to make it more efficient for everyone after the king's execution. Many enjoyed the new sense of freedom; society became more equal and ordered because of Puritanism. Furthermore, Jews, who had been expelled in 1290 as a result of religious intolerance, were invited back to Britain. Cromwell described the king's execution as a cruel necessity.

Key Words

regicide   purge   legislation

▼ SOURCE D *Adapted from* The History of the Rebellion, *by the Earl of Clarendon, published in 1702; this was the first full history of the civil war; Clarendon sat in parliament and was a supporter of the king:*

> It is most certain that, in that very hour when he was thus wickedly murdered in the sight of the sun, he was the worthiest gentleman, the best master and Christian.

▼ SOURCE E *Adapted from a contemporary pamphlet about Charles' death:*

> Even the crucifying of our blessed saviour did not equal this, and Christ was yet judged at a lawful court.

Work

1 a Write an account of the king's execution from either a royalist or a parliamentarian viewpoint. Think about key dates, times and people.
  b Swap books with someone who wrote from the other point of view. How are the accounts different?

2 Put the king on trial. In groups allocate roles and play out the trial of Charles I. Remember to focus on why he is being tried. Does everyone have the same reasons?

3 Parliament was right to sentence the king to death. How far do you agree?

Practice Question

Explain the significance of the execution of Charles I. **8 marks**

Study Tip

Try to explain that people at the time realised that the king's execution was a historic event.

5.4 How should Cromwell be remembered?

The Commonwealth was the name for the republic under the leadership of parliament after Charles' death. With Charles dead, the parliamentary army was the strongest force in the Commonwealth and its leader, Oliver Cromwell, the most powerful man. Cromwell is one of the most disputed characters in history. The opinions of him tend to change with shifting political events. When, in the nineteenth century, Britain moved towards a democracy and parliament became more important, historians became more sympathetic towards Cromwell. However, during the time of the restoration of the monarchy under Charles II, Cromwell was regularly depicted in royalist propaganda as the devil. Many people in Ireland have their own interpretations of Cromwell too. So how should he be remembered?

Objectives

- **Identify** the different views of Cromwell.
- **Analyse** the interpretations of Cromwell.
- **Compare** and contrast the Protectorate to earlier parliaments.

Fact

The Protectorate is the name given to the time when England, Scotland and Ireland did not have a monarch, but were ruled by Oliver Cromwell (and then his son). Sometimes this period is referred to as the Interregnum.

Cromwell and the Commonwealth

Positive views of Cromwell's rule?

There were many reasons people supported Cromwell. For example, he won wars against the Dutch and the Spanish and restored England's reputation abroad, and he introduced the Navigation Act in 1651, which stated that any ship coming into or leaving England had to be English. People were free to worship in any way they liked, and many ordinary people felt that Cromwell was on their side.

▼ **SOURCE A** *Samuel Cooper's painting of Cromwell, 1656. Cromwell is said to have told Cooper to paint him exactly as he saw him, 'warts and all'.*

▼ **SOURCE B** *Written by a bishop, 50 years after the Protectorate:*

Cromwell would rather have taken a shepherd's staff than the Protectorship. Nothing went more against his feelings than a show of greatness. But he saw it was necessary at that time to keep the nation from falling into extreme disorder.

▼ **SOURCE C** *Although Cromwell had always declined the Crown he was given a state burial on his death in 1658. This painting was produced in 1659. It shows Cromwell wearing the crown and holding the royal sceptre and orb.*

Negative views of Cromwell's rule?

Cromwell didn't please everyone. He appointed Major Generals to the 11 districts he created. People resented their presence because they kept such strict control on many aspects of life: they even tried to stop Christmas celebrations. The Levellers, a religious group who believed in equality, were imprisoned by Cromwell, and their leaders were killed. In Ireland, Cromwell laid siege to the town of Drogheda, and even when the townspeople surrendered he killed them – women and children included. Land was taken from Catholics in Ireland and given to Protestants, so England would always have allies in Ireland.

▼ SOURCE D *A Dutch drawing of Cromwell dressed as a king, with Charles I being executed in the background. The drawing was made at the time the Dutch were fighting a war against England.*

Positive or negative views of Cromwell's rule?

Some aspects of Cromwell's rule can be viewed as positive or negative! For example, Cromwell ended up with more power than Charles, and he secured his son as his successor. He felt that his victories since Naseby meant it was God's **providence** that he should be in charge, and sinful activities were banned to ensure that the Commonwealth was Godly.

Key Words

providence   radicalism

Challenges to the Commonwealth

There were many challenges to Cromwell's Protectorate and from this emerged a political and religious **radicalism** that had never existed before. The civil war saw the development of many Protestant groups, which would challenge Cromwell's authority. The biggest challenge came, however, from a political group. This group was the Levellers. They wanted a reform to political representation for the men who had fought in the New Model Army. Cromwell met with them and their leader, John Lilburne, during the Putney Debates in 1647 where their demands were heard. Support for them soon decreased and Lilburne was imprisoned. Cromwell was able to rule for 10 years.

The end of Cromwell and the Commonwealth

When Cromwell died in 1658 his son, Richard, took over the role. However, Richard was not interested in politics and resigned in 1659. In 1660, Charles II rode into London and was crowned king of England, Scotland and Ireland.

Cromwell's body was dug up from its grave and hung in Tyburn. His head was placed on a spike where it stayed for decades. Most people were happy to have a king back on the throne.

Work

1. a. Pick the top three things you think show Cromwell in a good light, and the top three things that show him in a bad light.
   b. Share your lists with your partner. Discuss your choices.
2. Study **Sources C** and **D**. Explain the impression that each one gives of Cromwell.

Practice Question

Explain two ways in which the achievements of the Protectorate and the rule of Simon de Montfort were similar. **8 marks**

Study Tip

Separate your points into political and religious outcomes and put all the key information into these factors. Think about how long they lasted and what kind of opposition they had.

6.1A What was the impact of the American Revolution?

Britain had become one of the most powerful countries during the seventeenth century and used this power to take over other parts of the world, including large parts of North America. However, by the mid-1700s the people of America no longer wanted to be part of the British **Empire**. They considered themselves American, and in the late 1700s fought a war against the British; and they won an unlikely victory. Why did these people want to be free of British rule?

Objectives

- **Explain** why the colonists in America were unhappy with British rule.
- **Analyse** the defeat of the British to show the consequences of this.
- **Compare** and contrast the revolution with past events.

Long-term causes of the American Revolution

In the sixteenth and early seventeenth centuries, groups of European settlers began to occupy land in North America – land owned by **indigenous Americans** (also known as Native Americans). After the British defeated the French and used their **colonies** there to make money, growing crops like cotton, tobacco and sugar to sell all over the world – often relying on **indentured servants** and, later, **enslaved** people (slaves). By the early 1700s, there were 13 separate English colonies in North America, and by 1775 the population of settlers and enslaved people was around 2.5 million.

Countries such as Britain wanted empires because they could tax the people who lived in the colonies, and ensure that they bought British goods. However, many of the **colonists** in America, despite being of British descent, now considered themselves American.

The American colonists started to resent the economic support they had to give to Britain. The British felt it was acceptable to tax the Americans to pay for the army, as the army 'protected' the colonists from other foreign powers, but the colonists objected. They were also unhappy about the Stamp Tax of 1765 (a tax on documents such as legal papers and newspapers), and responded by rioting. Throughout the 1760s, the colonists were also forced to comply with Navigation Acts, which ensured that only British goods were imported into America. There could be no trading with other countries. If Britain produced something, the colonists could not buy it from another country.

In addition, the colonists felt bossed about by the British because they were given boundaries on the land that they could not cross. The British had made these agreements with the indigenous Americans without consulting the colonists. These boundaries stopped them accessing good farmland: the colonists wanted to have more of a say.

No taxation without representation: short-term causes of the revolution

The American colonists were ruled directly from Britain yet they had no representatives in parliament in London. So they felt there was no one to speak up for them. Throughout this thematic study, from the barons to the working class, this is a common thread – the desire for representation. People wanted a voice in what was done to them and for them, especially if they were expected to pay for it through taxes! So the colonists, who had started to identify as American rather than as British, stated: No taxation without representation!

One key event considered the spark of the fight against the British was the Boston Massacre of 1770. When some anti-British colonists jeered, and threw snowballs and sticks at the British army on 5 March, the army opened fire and killed some of them. Unrest in Boston continued to grow when some of the colonists, unhappy with the heavily taxed British tea they were forced to buy, boarded a ship and poured the tea out into the harbour. This became known as the Boston Tea Party. This act of defiance scared the British and in retaliation they closed the port of Boston.

By 1775, anti-British feeling was so strong that when the British army tried to seize a supply of gunpowder in Concord they were fired on by 20,000 'minutemen'. These men were local farmers, clerks and ploughboys who had had enough of British rule. This became known as the Lexington incident and marked the start of the revolution against the British.

SOURCE A *A 1789 painting of the Boston Tea Party, showing Americans throwing the teaship cargoes into the river*

Declaration of Independence

The Americans were quick to organise themselves. They met in **Congress** to decide what to do, and by 1775 they had made George Washington the leader of their army.

In 1776, Congress had a meeting in Philadelphia where a Declaration of Independence was issued. This stated that the 13 colonies were free and that all control from Britain had ended. This was the easy step; the hard part would come in making the declaration a reality. There would be seven years of fighting before the colonists were victorious and an independent America was a reality.

SOURCE B *Adapted from the American Declaration of Independence, written by Thomas Jefferson in 1776:*

> We hold these truths to be self-evident, that all men are created equal, that they are endowed by their Creator with certain unalienable rights, that amongst these are Life, Liberty and the Pursuit of Happiness. That whenever any Government becomes destructive of these ends, it is the right of the people to alter or abolish it.

Fact

The Declaration of Independence, drawn up by white colonists, states that 'all men are created equal'. However, the declaration does not condemn or abolish slavery – in fact, the only mention of enslaved people is when it accuses the British of stirring up slave rebellions. In addition, the declaration shows the racist attitudes of the colonists as it refers to indigenous Americans as 'merciless Indian Savages'.

Key Words

indigenous American colony indentured servant enslaved colonist Congress

Extension

Look back to Chapter 1. In what ways is the American Declaration of Independence similar to Magna Carta? Do you think the Americans are right to compare the two? Think about the quote on the monument at Runnymede.

Work

1 a List the reasons why the colonists were dissatisfied with British rule. Use **Source B** to help you.
  b Colour code your reasons – the factors for unrest – into economic, social and political factors.

2 a What taxes were the colonists forced to pay?
  b In what ways did the colonists lack representation?
  c Do you think the British government understood how serious the colonists were?

3 a In your groups list the rules you would have in the Declaration of Independence.
  b How similar is your declaration to the section in **Source B**?

6.1B What was the impact of the American Revolution?

It would be astonishing if one of the biggest and best-trained armies in the world were to be defeated by a group of American farmers and clerks. How could this happen, and if it did, what would it mean for Britain's imperial power?

Yorktown and the defeat of the British

The British had won most of the battles during the American War of Independence. They had a world-class army that was well trained and well supplied. However, many of the battles took place in forest and mountain areas, in land the British did not know well.

▼ **C** *A map showing some of the War of Independence battles and the movements of the British, Americans and French that resulted in the British being trapped at Yorktown*

The decisive battle of the war was at Yorktown in 1781. The American troops, who were perceived to be weak, had reinforced themselves with 3000 extra men. Added to this they had the support of the French, who had secured control of the waters around Yorktown. This was important as the British needed to get their supplies in from the sea.

The British commander, Charles Cornwallis, unwittingly helped the Americans by moving his troops onto a **peninsula** as they awaited supplies. They were now cut off and in a weak position. George Washington, sensing the advantage he could have, attacked the British. With few weapons and no supplies the British were forced to surrender.

The battle at Yorktown saw the immediate defeat of the British and the end of the War of Independence. America was now an independent country, and proclaimed itself the 'land of the free'. This was an unprecedented victory. It showed what could be achieved with a clear cause against an opponent that underestimated your ability.

Fact

African-Americans were involved on both sides of the American Revolution – up to about 8000 on the side of the colonists, and about 20,000 for Britain. Most of them were enslaved people hoping for their freedom. Many indigenous peoples tried to stay neutral, but some tribes joined the war effort – most supporting the British in the hope that they would continue to restrict the expansion of the colonies.

Consequences for America

The Americans were delighted with their victory. Using their determination they had defeated the most powerful country in the world. However, not all of the people in America were happy with the outcome, and many moved north to Canada, which was still under the control of Britain.

The Americans set up their own system of government with a written set of rules (called a constitution), a parliament (Congress) and a President. This system still exists today. Americans now had the representation they desired. By the early twentieth century, America had developed into the most powerful independent country in the world.

However, the 'land of the free' was not perfect. Many poor farmers, who could not afford to buy their land, could not vote. Neither could African-Americans, indigenous Americans or women. Rich, white men were represented, but no one else. Slavery still existed and indigenous Americans were widely discriminated against, losing more land to the colonists: this was not equality.

Consequences for Britain

Britain had spent a lot of money on the war and had lost a lot of men. The involvement of France on the side of the revolution had worsened relations between the two powers. Britain was able to use the strength of its navy to make up for the loss of America by colonising other parts of the world. America had been used as a **penal colony**, where criminals were sent to work on the **plantations** alongside enslaved people and indentured servants who worked to pay off the cost of their passage across the Atlantic. Britain now turned its focus to Australia and New Zealand as a place to send convicts.

Relations with America improved as the years went by and the two countries started to trade with each other. The loss of America was not an issue by the late nineteenth century because by then Britain had a colony in every time zone of the world. The sun never set on the British Empire. And although America had once been considered the most important of the colonies it was soon replaced by India: the 'jewel in the crown'. The main problem for Britain's leaders was that the idea of overthrowing authority was one that might spread to Britain itself. With a growing working-class population this was possible.

Consequences for the world

The success of America and its fight against British authority inspired one of the most important events in European history. The French were fed up with their king, Louis XVI. People were starving while he and his wife ate lavish breakfasts and lived in luxurious palaces. The French people decided to take action, and the French Revolution began. There were many long-term factors that caused this revolution but the success of the American Revolution acted as a spark for the people of France to remove the **autocratic** rule of their king, Louis. This would go on to inspire the working class in Britain when it came to their voting rights and representation in parliament.

▼ **D** *The extent of the British Empire by 1921*

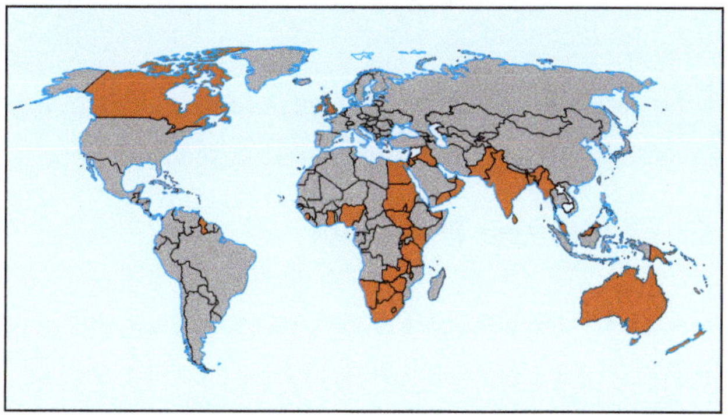

Key Words

peninsula penal colony
plantation autocratic

Work

1. Write a news report to explain how the British lost at Yorktown. Use the sources to help you add detail.
2. **a** What were the consequences of American Independence? Create a diagram showing this. You could have three circles, which show the economic, social and political consequences, or you can have a go at creating your own style of diagram.
   b Colour code your consequences to show long- and short-term ones.
   c Can you think of any other consequences for Britain?
3. Write a letter from George Washington to the British government, explaining how Britain should treat its new colonies across the world if it doesn't want another revolution. You should think about what had made the Americans so unhappy.
4. Create a grid for every revolt you have studied thus far. Have one column for similarities and one for differences. Which revolt do you think is most closely linked to the American Revolution?

Practice Question

Was the economy the main factor that caused the American Revolution?
16 marks
SPaG: 4 marks

Study Tip

You will need to explain your answer with reference to the economy and other factors. Think about using specific examples that strengthen your points. Can your examples support another judgement? Explain why they support your points more. The Boston Tea Party could support both economic and political factors so you have to use your evidence to say which it supports the most.

7.1A Give us the vote!

Since the thirteenth century, power had shifted between the monarch, the landowners and parliament. On a few occasions, when ordinary people had challenged the authority of those at the top (such as during the Peasants' Revolt), the challenge had never lasted and control of the country had ultimately remained in the hands of a very small minority. But in the nineteenth century, the Industrial Revolution created a large working class. They wanted, and demanded, representation. Did they use violent methods to try to achieve this? How did the government respond?

Objectives

- **Describe** the problems with voting rights before the early nineteenth century.
- **Explain** the forms of protest for voting reform.
- **Analyse** the impact of the Great Reform Act.

The problem with who could vote

In the early nineteenth century, the king and those who owned land and titles were the people who controlled the country. They made decisions about how the country should be run and what should happen to everyone else in society. This became a problem when the population increased during the Industrial Revolution. Many factory owners became very wealthy – but they, and their workers, had no political power.

One of the main complaints was about the so-called rotten boroughs. These were areas that sent two Members of Parliament (MPs) to parliament even though no one lived there. In one case there was a mound of grass, called Old Sarum, where a village used to be: still, two MPs went to parliament to represent it! Birmingham, on the other hand, was one of the largest and fastest growing towns, yet it had no MPs to represent its people in parliament. Pocket boroughs were also an issue. These were boroughs that were controlled by rich individuals who did not represent the needs of everyone.

When people did go to vote there was no secret **ballot**. This meant that people had to say in public who they were voting for. Therefore, they could be easily bribed, and in some cases people were sacked if they did not vote for the 'right' candidate. This was not true representation, as the same corrupt people continued to hold the power.

Unfairly, some people were allowed to vote purely because they had a fireplace and a locked door! These were called potwalloper boroughs because in order to prove their assets, the men would rattle their keys in a large cooking pot. On top of all of this, women did not have the vote. Despite how much money, how many fireplaces and how many locked doors they had!

▼ **SOURCE A** *A painting by William Hogarth, from 1755, called* The Polling; *it shows disabled men being helped up the stairs to vote for a particular candidate*

Radical protest

In Britain, both rich and poor alike noted the effect of the French Revolution, an event in which the ordinary people of France rebelled violently against the ruling class. This coincided with the end of the Battle of Waterloo, when many soldiers were returning home and needed work. The introduction of Corn Laws and a poor harvest meant people were starving. People were now no longer in a position to wait for change – they needed representation in parliament, and radical speakers started to demand it.

Case Study: Peterloo

In 1819, there was a gathering in St Peter's Fields, in Manchester, of people who were demanding the vote. This was a peaceful protest where the 60,000 protestors listened to speeches by radicals such as

Henry Hunt. Hunt inspired the crowds with his speech that called for the reform of parliament.

The local magistrate panicked when he heard how many people had gathered, and called the local militia in. It is reported that they were drunk, and so events escalated quickly. Within ten minutes, 600 people had been wounded and 15 had been killed. These figures included women and children. Working-class people making clear demands had scared the authorities into responding with violence.

After the event, which became known as the Peterloo Massacre, the government introduced the Six Acts. These stated that any meeting of more than 50 people for radical reform was an act of treason. Anyone doing this was now breaking the law.

▼ **SOURCE B** ***This is the official plaque that was put up in Manchester to commemorate the events at Peterloo. Many people felt it did not reflect the true events, and it made no mention of the people killed.***

▼ **SOURCE C** ***This alternative plaque replaced the blue plaque in 2007. It gives a more accurate account of the events at Peterloo.***

Key Word

ballot

▼ **SOURCE D** ***An 1819 painting called* The Massacre of Peterloo*, showing Henry Hunt and his supporters waving the revolutionary flag of France. You can see women and children being attacked by the soldiers on their horses.***

Work

1. **a** Who was allowed to vote in the early nineteenth century?
   b How does **Source A** support your list of who could vote? Can you spot the woman in the distance? Why might she be painted far away?
   c Can you see any other problems with the voting system, from the details given in the painting?
2. Write a letter to the Prime Minister in 1819 describing the reasons why there should be voting reform.
3. List the key differences between **Source B** and **Source C**.
4. **a** Explain the key features of radical protest for voting reform. Use the sources to help you.
   b Which of **Source B**, **Source C** and **Source D** is the most accurate as a piece of evidence about the events at Peterloo? Explain your answer.

Extension

GCSE

A public survey voted the events at Peterloo as more significant than the Putney Debates (see page 41). In groups, carry out more research on both and create a presentation that states whether you agree or disagree.

7.1B Give us the vote!

So far, nothing had changed for working-class people, or for the middle classes. They still needed change, but instead of protesting they now tried to convince the government to change things and extend the franchise (give more people the vote) through legislation.

Who was in charge?

The political party that had been in charge at the beginning of the nineteenth century was the **Tory** party, who were against reform. They were voted out of government in 1830 and replaced by the **Whig** party, led by Earl Grey.

This coincided with the death of King George IV. He had been considered insane and had not been running the country well: he was extravagant and was not interested in making life better for ordinary people. George was replaced by King William IV in 1830, who was more open to reform and improving society.

How did people try to convince the king?

The government had cracked down on public gatherings and protests for change. However, a Birmingham man called Thomas Attwood formed the Birmingham Political Union of the Lower and Middle Classes of People in 1829. Attwood, along with 8000 others, sent a **petition** to parliament for reform. They wanted shorter parliaments, the end of property qualifications and a vote for all men who contributed to local or national taxes. However, the petition was rejected.

▼ **SOURCE E** **The Meeting of the Birmingham Political Union,** *painted in 1832–33 by Benjamin Robert Haydon*

By the end of 1829, the union was renamed the Birmingham Political Union (BPU). The group vowed to cooperate with the law – this would make it harder for the BPU to be banned – and it was agreed that the lower and middle classes would unite for the cause.

The BPU model was copied around the country, so when Attwood called for people not to pay their taxes, the king and the government started to worry.

The Great Reform Act, 1832

Earl Grey's Whig government tried to pass laws for a reform act. In fact they tried three times to get a reform act through! This is how the system works: when the government wants to pass a law, they have to send it through the House of Lords. The House of Lords is the part of parliament that is not elected. In the first parliament – the Great Council – they were the barons and nobles. So, can you see the problem? The House of Lords did not want to pass an act that would give more power to the ordinary people by having them represented in parliament.

On the third attempt, Earl Grey went to the king and requested that lords be appointed who were Whigs, or at least sympathetic to reform. The existing lords were horrified at the idea, because it would mean that Tory lords would lose some of their power to the Whigs, so they passed the Reform Act in 1832. It had been such a fight to get the act passed that it was called the Great Reform Act.

How great was the Great Reform Act?

The middle class did well out of the Great Reform Act. Merchants and industrialists gained more representation and were happier that their interests were being considered. Rotten boroughs were removed and new towns, such as Birmingham, were allowed to elect MPs. The working class, however, were unhappy about the Reform Act being called 'Great'. They had not been given the vote, as most only earned around £50 a year. There was no secret ballot until 1872, so the lucky few working-class people who could actually vote were

SOURCE F *This painting, by Sir George Hayte in 1833, hangs in the National Portrait Gallery. It shows key individuals involved in the Great Reform Act of 1832.*

G *The main points of the Great Reform Act*

- 56 very small locations lose the right to elect their own MPs
- 30 other smaller towns lose one MP
- London and other large towns and cities are given more MPs
- People who earn £150 a year can vote
- Voters increase from 435,000 to 652,000

effectively forced to vote for their factory or landowner, rather than their chosen candidate. The act meant that only one in seven men could vote; this didn't represent the people of Britain.

The Reform Act did not change things for working-class people in the short term. However, it had been proven that change was possible, and over the next decades the call for further parliamentary reform continued. Furthermore, the Reform Act reduced the power of the king and landowners. The middle class had joined the electorate: they now had influence and this could only mean more change.

Key Words

Tory Whig petition

Work

1 Create and complete a table with two headings: People who opposed reform; People who supported reform.

2 How did the BPU try to convince the government to extend the franchise?

3 a The National Portrait Gallery paid a lot of money for **Source F**. Was it worth the money? Should the Great Reform Act be remembered?

b Write a letter to the National Portrait Gallery explaining your judgement.

Practice Question

Explain two ways in which Peterloo and the Newport rising (see page 51) were similar.

8 marks

Study Tip

Remember in your answer to explain the reasons for, the development of and the consequences of each event.

7.2A What was the impact of Chartism?

Working-class men had fought hard and supported the campaign for reform in 1832. However, they were left feeling bitter after the Great Reform Act: they were still unable to vote because they did not qualify under new rules that said voters must own property worth at least £10. Lots of other factors came together to fuel further unrest. Through the anger, the **Chartist movement** was born. The Chartists were a group of like-minded people with clear aims that focused around equal representation for the working class. What specifically did the Chartists want, and how did they go about getting it? Did the Whig government support the movement?

Objectives

- **Describe** the aims of the Chartists.
- **Examine** the tactics of the Chartists.
- **Evaluate** the impact the Chartists had.

Poor harvests and the Poor Law

Working-class people were becoming more and more disgruntled due to their poor living and working conditions. They found it hard to find work because of the new machines being invented: one machine could do the work of ten men, and faster. This meant that most jobs no longer required skill; even children could do them. The Industrial Revolution had created problems that the government needed to solve, and so it reformed the Poor Law in 1834. This was done through a desire to help people in the new industrial society, by offering help to those who struggled financially. People who needed Poor Law assistance would be sent to the workhouse: this was seen as help at the time. However, this did not solve the problems faced by most people. Bad harvests in the 1830s added to the troubles of the poor. When were the working class going to get the help and representation they deserved?

William Lovett and the birth of the Chartist movement

In 1836, the Chartist movement was born when William Lovett, from the London Working Men's Association, started a campaign that was quickly adopted around the country. Thomas Attwood and the Birmingham Political Union joined the campaign. This led to a national Chartist convention being held in Birmingham in 1839.

The movement was a peaceful one, due to Lovett's Christian faith, and organised the mass signing of petitions to be sent to parliament. The Chartists had six main aims, set out in a document called the People's Charter.

▼ **A** *The demands of the People's Charter*

The demands would make voting, and therefore society, fairer. If MPs were paid then working-class people could become MPs. They could then promote the interests of the working class in parliament. This was truly a charter for equality. In 1839, the first petition was sent to parliament. However, it was rejected.

SOURCE B *Adapted from a speech by William Lovett, before 1839:*

> Let us, friends, seek to join together the honest, moral, hardworking and intelligent member of society. Let us find out our rights from books. Let us collect information about our lives, our wages and our conditions. Then let us publish our views. Then MPs will agree there must be change, without having to use violence and arrest.

Moral force or physical force?

The rejection of the petition was a real blow to the Chartist movement and some supporters decided that peaceful methods of protest were not enough. Chartists in South Wales, for example, were particularly angered by the rejection. Here, unemployment was higher than average and many people were starving. They decided to march on Newport in November 1839. One of their leaders had been imprisoned and many planned to attack the prison and free him. However, when they reached Newport the authorities were ready for them, and had soldiers guarding the prison. The soldiers opened fire and 22 men were killed. The attack was over.

By 1842, another petition was being sent to parliament. This also coincided with the emergence of Feargus O'Connor. He became the undisputed leader of the movement when the 1842 petition was rejected, and called for violent actions to pressurise parliament into agreeing to the demands. Many workers in factories in the north of England started to vandalise machinery. These actions became known as the 'plug plot'. They demonstrated that people would stop at nothing to get the charter passed through parliament.

O'Connor called for a **general strike** of all workers and even went as far as calling for a British republic. He was determined to remove the people who kept working men down. The government became so concerned it moved Queen Victoria to the Isle of Wight, for her own safety.

By 1847, the economic and agricultural **depression** had returned to Britain. There was a surge in support for the Chartists. A third petition was signed and taken to parliament. Did it succeed?

Key Words

Chartist movement | general strike | depression

Work

1. a Write a list of the six aims of the Chartists.
   b Beside each aim, write what it would change.
   c Which aim do you think would have the most impact?
2. Create a conversation between Lovett and O'Connor. They should be trying to convince each other of their tactics. Use examples of successes and failures that could support their points.
3. Group discussion: Who do you think had the right idea? Which tactics worked better?

SOURCE C *A sketch by John Leech that appeared in* Punch *magazine in 1849*

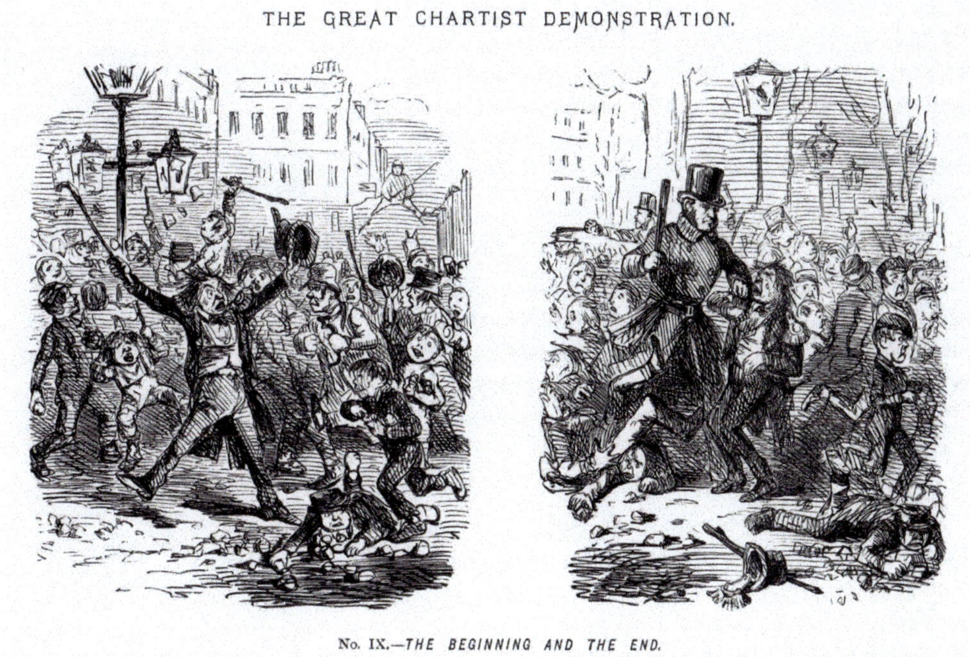

7.2B What was the impact of Chartism?

The Chartists were divided between those who believed in moral force and those who believed that physical force was the solution. Also, there were many other areas of life, in addition to politics, that the Chartists wanted to reform. But did they achieve their six main aims, as set out in the People's Charter?

Other areas of reform

Lovett was committed to education and reform through the cooperative movement. This movement was inspired by Robert Owen (see page 62) and helped bring a better standard of living to working-class communities. Many Chartists became heavily involved in the **trade union** movements that would become important in the latter half of the century.

Lovett and other leaders also promoted **temperance**. This is zero tolerance of alcohol and was a popular movement in the early nineteenth century. It was believed that parliament would have to take the Chartists seriously if they were sober. This would show that working-class people were disciplined and worthy of the vote.

O'Connor was interested in land reform. He felt that everyone was entitled to land, and that if they had land, they could leave the factory towns and the problems they faced there. There were several sites where this kind of land reform took place, and one of the most significant was named 'O'Connorville'. The scheme worked for a while but the land was poorly farmed by the settlers and eventually the scheme failed. Despite their differences, it is clear both that Lovett and O'Connor wanted to improve life for the working class.

Government responses

The government feared the Chartists, who were able to mobilise large groups of people from all classes. In addition, they had respectable leaders, and even a newspaper, the *Northern Star*, which they could use to promote their agenda. The government took decisive action against them, in addition to rejecting their petitions. Local government officials put up posters in towns asking people not to attend Chartist meetings. They would freely arrest Chartists, with Lovett and O'Connor being arrested on more than one occasion.

One tool the government used to deter people from pushing for reform was transportation. It had been decided that the death penalty was too harsh for many crimes. Therefore, people were transported to other countries, such as Australia, as punishment. This threat from the government was enough to dissuade people from joining the Chartist movement.

Fact

William Cuffay was a black man who was the son of a formerly enslaved person. An important Chartist leader in London, Cuffay supported physical force. He was transported to Australia for his activities, where he quickly set up Chartist groups to support the freedom of indigenous people. The Chartist movement spread around the empire, where others, like Cuffay, were transported. Chartism continued to challenge the British government even on different continents!

One of the most significant actions by the government was when the third Chartist petition was taken to parliament in 1848.

The end of Chartism?

O'Connor and fewer than 50,000 supporters met on Kennington Common in London on 10 April 1848. Expecting more, the Duke of Wellington had prepared troops and police. Some 85,000 special constables were

▼ **SOURCE D** *The Great Chartist Meeting at Kennington Common, 10 April 1848, just before the presentation of the third Chartist petition. This image is an early photograph called a daguerreotype, which usually reversed the image. The technology was replaced by easier methods after 1860.*

enrolled for the day: they were not going to let O'Connor and his followers disturb London.

Wellington stopped the crowd from entering the city, and O'Connor was forced to take the petition into London himself. The petition was said to have over five million signatures: in fact it had fewer than two million.

The petition was read out in parliament and it transpired that thousands of the signatures were forged. Many were seemingly from Queen Victoria herself! O'Connor argued that this was because workers had to keep their identity a secret from their employers. Parliament saw the whole thing as a farce.

The Chartist movement was not a complete disaster, as in the end all but one of the six aims in the People's Charter were achieved by 1928.

Why did the Chartist movement fail in the short term?

There are many reasons why the Chartist movement failed to have an immediate impact. There was strong parliamentary opposition, with clear strategies being used; mainly government suppression of local meetings and gatherings. The standard of living started to increase during the 1850s and there were many alternative working-class movements such as trade unionism and cooperatives. The divided leadership of Lovett and O'Connor was certainly a cause of failure. Without one clear message, and with too many fringe groups, the movement was doomed to failure.

▼ **SOURCE E** *A cartoon published in* Punch *magazine, May 1859, mocking the petition*

Key Words

trade union temperance

▼ **F** *The Chartist aims and the dates they were met*

Votes for all men!
1918

Equal-sized constituencies!
1884

Voting in secret!
1872

Wages for MPs!
1911

No property qualifications to be able to vote!
1918 (men)

An election every year!
Never

Work

1. a. Which tactics did the government use to defeat the Chartists?
   b. Which tactic had the biggest impact?
2. a. What is the message of the cartoon in **Source E**?
   b. Why was this cartoon created?
3. Do you think **Source E** is useful as evidence of why Chartism failed?
4. Create your own cartoon showing another reason for the failure of Chartism.

Practice Question

How useful is **Source D** to a historian studying support for the Chartists? **8 marks**

Study Tip

Refer in your answer to the type of source it is and what it shows.

8.1 The Anti-Corn Law League

The early nineteenth century had seen a number of reform movements. There were campaigns to change voting rules, to end slavery and to improve living and working conditions, for example. At the same time another movement developed, called the Anti-Corn Law League. This group campaigned over the price of wheat, which was a very contentious issue in the nineteenth century. So why were there laws about wheat at this time? What methods did the Anti-Corn Law League use? Did it change the lives of poor people?

Objectives

- **Identify** the reasons the Corn Laws were passed.
- **Analyse** the factors that led to the repeal of the Corn Laws.
- **Evaluate** the impact of the Anti-Corn Law league.

Fact

The price of wheat affected everyone because it was used to make bread – a staple food for many people.

What were the Corn Laws?

Britain had been at war with France (1803–15) and thus had stopped trading with the French. During the war, British farmers had the monopoly on wheat sales and the prices soared. When the war ended there were calls to start trading with France, which had cheaper wheat. However, the politicians in government were wealthy landowners. They had made money from the high wheat prices and were reluctant to see their profits fall. So, the government passed the Corn Laws in 1815. These laws were designed to keep the price of wheat high. If the price fell too low, imports of wheat would be stopped. This kept the wealthy landowners and farmers happy, but were the manufacturers and workers happy?

Why and how did the 'Leaguers' protest?

Many people were unhappy with the Corn Laws and their impact on the price of bread. There were riots up and down the country, from Westminster to Dundee, as the Corn Laws made their way through parliament.

The Anti-Corn Law League was mostly made up of middle-class men who felt that the restrictions were unfair to the poor and the manufacturing middle class. Two prominent 'Leaguers' were Richard Cobden and John Bright. Both men were excellent **orators** and toured the country, giving speeches and spreading support for the league. They created pamphlets and published articles in sympathetic newspapers. They were quick to take advantage of new technology by using the railway to travel faster, and spreading their pamphlets through the penny post: this was a cheap post that most people could afford. They used it to send a pamphlet to every eligible voter in the country, and easily obtained nationwide support. Their main arguments were:

- The laws were unfair to the poor because they increased the price of a basic food – bread!
- Cheap wheat could help to lower living costs.
- People could spend more money on other foods, such as meat, which would help farmers.
- People could also spend more money on industrial goods, thus benefiting the manufacturers.
- Countries that could export their wheat to Britain would have the money to invest in industry.
- The relationship built up through trade with these countries could ensure peace in Europe in the coming years.

The league had a lot of support, which increased when both Cobden and Bright were elected as MPs, in 1841 and 1843 respectively. In parliament they found the support of the new Prime Minister, Robert Peel.

Peel was a supporter of **free trade** and saw the benefits of **repealing** the Corn Laws. However, he was also the leader of the Conservative Party, whose members were mostly wealthy landowners: they would not support changes to a law which protected their wealth.

SOURCE A *Adapted from a quote by an MP in Scotland, Joseph Hume, in the 1830s:*

> Every man who earns his bread by his labour, should raise his voice against the Corn Laws, as they produce stagnation in trade, a want of work, and starvation.

Famine and crop failure: other factors for reform

There had been attempts at reforming the Corn Laws in the 1820s but none had done enough for the poor and starving of Britain. It would be the plight of the poor that would eventually push Peel's dithering hand.

In the early 1840s, there was a potato failure in Ireland. This was caused by the crop disease blight, which had spread across Europe. This was a problem for the poor in Ireland as they relied heavily on potatoes and bread for their diet. By 1846, Ireland was experiencing a terrible famine and millions of people were starving. The Corn Laws meant that there was no spare wheat to send to Ireland. Something had to be done.

Simultaneously, there were crop failures in England and Scotland and reports of suffering started to reach London. The bad harvest, the lack of work for **tenant farmers** and the high price of bread was about to cause a similar crisis to the one in Ireland.

Corn Laws repealed

In 1846, Robert Peel repealed the Corn Laws. In his final speech in parliament, he stated that he hoped people would remember him as someone who did the right thing. It is fair to say that he understood the problems faced by the Chartists and the workers; he did change conditions for the workers. But in doing so, he faced so much backlash from his own political party that he had to resign. He would never hold office again.

Impact of repeal

The repealing of the Corn Laws did not have the devastating effect on wheat prices as anticipated. What British farmers hadn't realised was that the low price of wheat after the end of the war with France was not because of foreign imports but because of wheat over-production in Britain during the war years.

The increase in population and the return to normal prices of wheat meant that farmers and landowners did not suffer. The poor were able to afford wheat and the price of barley, oats and meat actually increased, which helped those farmers who had been affected.

Many historians argue that the influence of the landowning class was challenged by the repeal of the Corn Laws and led to more protection for the working class in future years.

Key Words

orator free trade repeal tenant farmer

▼ **SOURCE B** *A drawing seen in the* Illustrated London News, *December 1849, showing an Irish woman, Bridget O'Donnel, with her children; they are starving because of the famine*

Work

1 a Who would benefit from the Corn Laws? Why?
  b What did the Corn Laws mean for the working class?

2 Write a speech for a public meeting about the Corn Laws. You want to persuade people to vote against them. Pick the three best arguments and focus on them in your speech.

3 Explain the importance of the famine in Ireland in influencing the repeal of the Corn Laws.

Practice Question

Explain two ways in which the Anti-Corn Law League and the Chartists were similar. **8 marks**

Study Tip

Explain your answer with reference to both the Anti-Corn Law League and the Chartists.

8.2A What was the impact of the anti-slavery movement?

From the 1500s onwards, Britain had made money from slavery. However, in the nineteenth century, Britain's involvement in the slave trade stopped. There were several reasons for this. For example, enslaved people had rebelled against slavery for many years, which changed the way people thought about the slave trade, and people campaigned to abolish slavery until Britain made it illegal to own slaves in 1833. So why was Britain involved in the slave trade? And who led the anti-slavery movement?

Objectives

- **Identify** the motivations for Britain's involvement in slavery.
- **Explain** the factors that led to the end of slavery.
- **Make** a judgement on why slavery ended and the consequences of this.

What was the slave trade?

Britain had been involved in slavery since the fifteenth century. For hundreds of years, British traders had made money by selling people to work in the Caribbean and then America. Some enslaved people were brought to Britain to work too. The British, along with other European nations, had set up plantations growing mainly cotton and sugar; they needed people to pick the crops. They got their enslaved people from the west coast of Africa. There, many tribal leaders were happy to sell people to the slave traders. In return they were given goods such as cloth, guns, glass and iron.

Britain made lots of money from slavery. Evidence of this can be seen in cities such as Bristol, Liverpool and Glasgow, where houses and iconic buildings were built using money made through the slave trade.

Life as an enslaved person

Conditions were dreadful on the ships that took enslaved Africans across the Atlantic. The men, women and children were crammed in on top of each other. On average, one third of the passengers died on each crossing.

▶ **SOURCE A** *William Cunninghame, who made his fortune from tobacco plantations, built this grand mansion in 1870. Today the building is Glasgow's Gallery of Modern Art.*

When the ships arrived at their destinations, the enslaved people were treated like animals during the auctions, where people bid for them. Life on the plantations was extremely difficult. Enslaved people were expected to work all their lives; if they didn't work hard enough or tried to escape they would be severely punished. They had no legal rights. Their average life expectancy was 27.

▼ **SOURCE B** *A drawing from 1787, which appeared in newpapers, pamphlets, books and posters, showing the cramped conditions endured by enslaved people on slave ships. This ship, the* Brookes*, had 454 people crammed into its hold.*

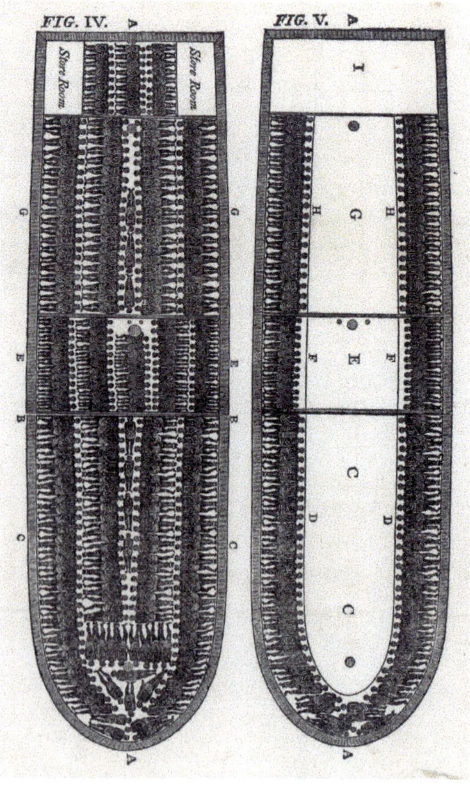

Abolition movement: William Wilberforce and friends

After hundreds of years of slavery, many people started to accept that it was wrong. One of the main motivations for this new view was the comparison to the working conditions in the factories; the workers had been referred to as 'white slaves'. It became clear that if they opposed the horrible conditions of the British factories, they should also oppose slavery. Others were led by their religious convictions that slavery was not Christian. One group that believed this was led by William Wilberforce. He, and likeminded others, created the Anti-Slavery Society.

The society held public meetings to educate people, they produced pamphlets and posters, and society members wore a badge to display their membership. These actions were designed to raise awareness and show support for the abolition of the slave trade. Different Anti-Slavery Society members made different contributions to the cause.

Many working-class people supported the movement, with workers in Manchester signing a petition to parliament. By 1792, a quarter of the population of Manchester had signed the petition.

▼ **SOURCE C** *The badge of the Society for the Abolition of Slavery, designed by the famous pottery owner Josiah Wedgwood in 1787*

Key Word

bill

William Wilberforce:

- MP for Hull
- motivated by his Christian faith
- spoke in parliament and pushed several **bills** through to abolish slavery
- held meetings to convince other prominent members of society to end slavery, and in 1797, presented a petition to parliament – it had more signatures than the Chartist petition
- secured the Abolition of the Slave Trade Act in 1807, which made it illegal to buy and sell enslaved people in the British Empire (but people were allowed to keep the enslaved people they already owned).

Olaudah Equiano:

- had been enslaved to a ship-master and had travelled the world, during which time he was educated and converted to Christianity
- bought his freedom and travelled more before settling in England
- was a prominent abolitionist; wrote a book, *The Interesting Narrative of the Life of Olaudah Equiano or Gustavus Vassa, the African* (1789)
- his autobiography was used by the abolition movement to win people's support: it made people aware of the horrors of slavery.

Thomas Clarkson:

- collected information about slavery and the conditions on board slave ships
- considered slavery evil and saw it as his job to do something about it
- produced drawings of the conditions on slave ships and pamphlets to show how horrible the conditions were for enslaved people.

Granville Sharp:

- in the late 1700s, supported cases of black enslaved people in Britain who wanted to be free
- motivated by his studies and his interest in politics and law
- in the famous case of Jonathan Strong, who was recaptured by his former slavemaster and sent back to the Caribbean, Sharp won his case for freedom
- his work showed how unclear the law was in Britain about owning enslaved people
- brought to public attention the case of the slave ship *Zong*, where 133 enslaved people were reportedly thrown overboard.

Work

1. List three reasons why Britain was involved in slavery. What do you think was the most important reason?
2. **a** Can you think of two categories that the motivations of the abolitionists fit into?
   b Use your categories as headings and write all the methods they used to end slavery below these.

8.2B What was the impact of the anti-slavery movement?

Wilberforce and his supporters campaigned for the end of slavery for years. It was finally abolished by the British parliament in 1807, making it illegal to buy and sell people – though those who were already owned did not have to be freed. In 1833, parliament banned slave ownership throughout the empire and the government agreed to pay former slave owners £20 million for their 'loss of property'. For example, the Bishop of Exeter received over £12,000 for the loss of 665 enslaved people.

Anti-abolitionists

The abolition movement was not fully supported within government. This was because many of the MPs and lords had made their money from slavery, or a link to it. If slavery ended, plantation owners would have to pay their workers and this would mean they could lose money.

Slave-trade supporters created propaganda supporting the view that black people were inferior, and that Britain had a responsibility to keep enslaved black people locked up. This was called the 'white man's burden'.

▼ **SOURCE D** *A 1789 cartoon by William Dent opposing the abolition of slavery; the heads at the bottom are 'Abolition' (labelled 'Folly') and 'Regulation' (labelled 'Wisdom'). The cartoon argues that regulation of the slave trade would be better than abolition.*

Women and the abolition movement

Despite women not yet having the vote, and playing little role in politics, many women got involved in the abolition movement. One of these was Hannah More, who wrote poems for the movement. More met Wilberforce in 1787 and they formed a firm friendship, based around their faith and commitment to social reform.

There were many anti-slavery societies run by women; in fact, by the time slavery was abolished in 1833, there were 73 such organisations. They were located across the whole of Britain, demonstrating that women nationwide were concerned about the issue of slavery and were willing to take action.

▼ **SOURCE E** *Adapted from Hannah More's poem,* Slavery, *written in 1788:*

> Was it decreed, fair Freedom! At thy birth,
> That thou should never irradiate all the earth?
> While Britain basks in thy full blaze of light,
> Why lies sad Africa quenched in total night?

Resistance by enslaved people

The abolition of slavery was not achieved only by middle-class white people in Britain. Enslaved people had been resisting slavery for many years and these rebellions changed the way people thought about the slave trade.

When the British took control of Jamaica in 1655, the **Maroons** escaped from the plantations where they were forced to work and went to live in the mountains. The British knew that if word spread of this group, they would face slave rebellions everywhere. Thus, they negotiated with the Maroons, and managed to control rebellions for a time.

It was harder to suppress rebellions after the French Revolution spread new ideas of freedom and equality. Two years after the revolution, the enslaved people of St Dominique, a French-controlled island, rebelled. They killed the white plantation owners and burnt the sugar crops. The French and British tried to stop this rebellion, but failed. This was partly because of the brilliant leadership of Toussaint L'Ouverture. He led fellow enslaved people to victory and slavery was abolished on the island in 1804. The island was declared independent and given the new name Haiti.

The rebellions sent a clear message that enslaved people were not willing to accept slavery, and expected more from life. They proved they would use any means to gain freedom.

The economic factors of abolition

Some historians now argue that the abolition of slavery was less to do with a surge of social consciousness, and more to do with a decline in the economic benefits of slavery. In other words, slavery was making less money than it used to! Sugar could be imported more cheaply from Brazil and Cuba; there was no need for the British to grow it themselves.

Was the abolition movement a complete success?

The Abolition of Slavery Act 1833 only instantly freed enslaved people under the age of six. The rest were put into age categories and were promised freedom after four years. William Wilberforce has been widely criticised for supporting this staged abolition. He argued that enslaved people had not been educated and needed to be trained to live outside the shackles of slavery. Many others disagreed with this strategy and campaigned for the immediate release of all enslaved people.

The road to freedom was not smooth. Many enslaved people were sacked if they refused to live in their old quarters. Smuggling of enslaved people became a problem: as it was done in secret, it made conditions even worse as there was no one to **regulate** it. The smuggling was carried out by former slave traders who did not want to give up the money they could make from slavery. For many enslaved people, freedom led to a decline in living standards as they tried to compete for work and wages.

In the long term the success of the abolition movement was undoubtedly a positive change for black people globally, as Britain increased the pressure on other nations to abolish slavery.

▼ **SOURCE F** *Adapted from a book,* The Black Jacobins, *written in 1938 by an African-Caribbean historian, C. L. R. James:*

> Those who see in the abolition of slavery the awakening conscience of mankind should spend a few minutes asking themselves why it is that man's conscience, which has slept peacefully for so many centuries, should awaken just at the time that men began to see the unprofitableness of slavery.

Practice Question

How useful is **Source D** to a historian studying the anti-slavery campaign? **8 marks**

Key Word

Maroons regulate

Extension

In 2001, the World Conference against Racism met in South Africa. One member addressed the conference to say that he wanted Britain and the other nations involved in the slave trade to admit that slavery was a crime against humanity. He also called for compensation for the descendants of enslaved people and nations that had been impacted by slavery. Britain refused to do either. The debate for compensation found support again in 2015. Research the various groups campaigning for this and create a presentation saying whether you agree or disagree.

Work

1. Complete the diagram below to explain how each factor led to abolition. In the parts that overlap put events that could be linked to more than one factor.
2. Which factor do you think had the most impact? Explain your decision.
3. Imagine it is the 200-year anniversary of the abolition of slavery. Write a post for your school's website explaining the impact the acts of 1807 and 1833 had.

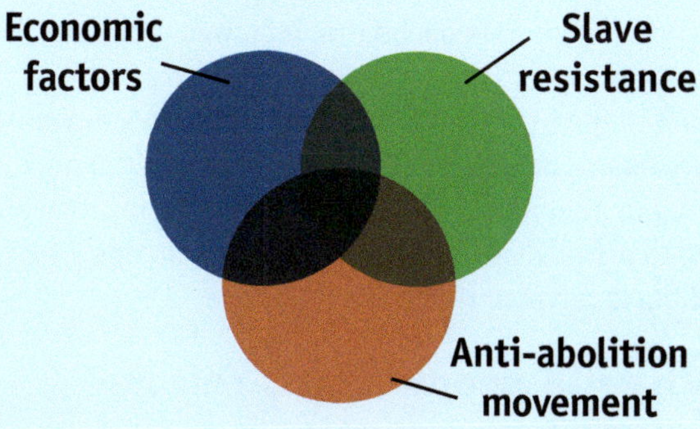

Study Tip

Write about what the cartoonist wants you to think about the opposition to the anti-slavery campaign. Why is the date of the cartoon important? Explain your answer.

8.3A Factory and social reform

The Industrial Revolution started around 1750. Before this, most people had worked at home, in the 'Domestic System'; this normally involved the whole family. They had managed their own time and took breaks when they wanted. With the building of factories and the demand these created for coal, working conditions changed. The new factories were often dangerous, noisy, dirty buildings, controlled by factory owners and managers who were more concerned with making money than with the health and wellbeing of their workforce. Several people campaigned to try to improve working conditions in factories. How did people react to reform, and did it make life better for everyone? How successful were the reformers?

Objectives

- **Describe** attitudes to reform in the nineteenth century.
- **Explore** the results of factory and social reform.
- **Analyse** the impact of reform on society.

Factory conditions

Textiles such as woollen and cotton cloth were the main products being made in factories in Britain during the Industrial Revolution. The factories were built because the new machines that made production more efficient, cheaper and quicker were too big for people's homes. With the new factories came new, longer working hours and new dangers. Children as young as six worked in some factories. Accidents were common, in which young people might lose limbs and, in extreme cases, their lives.

Mine conditions – a family affair

Coal mines provided jobs for the whole family. Men manually cut the coal away from the **coal seam**, and women worked as bearers carrying the coal to the surface. Children had jobs that matched their age. Older boys would push the coal in carts from the coal seam to the bearers. Children as young as four would work as trappers. They would have to sit in the dark for up to 12 hours a day, opening the door for the carts and to provide ventilation. Many lost their legs when the carts ran over them.

Why did people want reform?

The public were horrified when they heard about the conditions people worked in. Men's work was hard but people were shocked when they heard about women and children. Reports started to come from inspectors and from those who supported the reform of working conditions. One supporter was an MP called Michael Sadler. His report showed that factory children were being caught under machines and injured, and were being mistreated by factory owners. Because of this, Sadler suggested that those under 18 years old should not be allowed to work more than 10 hours a day; this became known as the 10-hour movement. Other reports highlighted that girls were carrying baskets of coal weighing up to 150 kilogrammes, and that women were dragging carts of coal on their hands and knees. Most people were appalled.

Lord Shaftesbury was another keen reformer. He made it his personal mission to improve the lives of children both at work and socially. He wanted reforms to apply

▼ **SOURCE A** *A drawing from 1881 that appeared in the* Illustrated London News, *showing a government inspector visiting a factory where children are employed*

to all factories, not just textile factories. He was led by his Christian beliefs and what he felt was the humane way to treat people, regardless of their social status. Shaftesbury, like Sadler, gave support to the 10-hour movement; he was also an important supporter of the Mines Act of 1842 and a campaigner for more education for children who worked in factories.

It is important to remember that the campaign for the abolition of slavery was happening at the same time: people started to refer to the factory workers as 'white slaves'.

Why were people against reform?

Many people were against reform because of **laissez-faire** politics. This was the belief that politics should not be involved in people's personal lives. In terms of factory reform, it was believed that working conditions were a private arrangement between a person and his or her employer. In terms of social reform – making people's lives better outside the workplace – there was a belief that people were poor because of their own bad choices. Why should the rich have to pay for the poor when they were feckless and undeserving?

▼ **SOURCE B** *A portrait of Lord Shaftesbury, Anthony Ashley-Cooper*

Key Words

coal seam   laissez-faire

▼ **C** *Some points of the acts for reform*

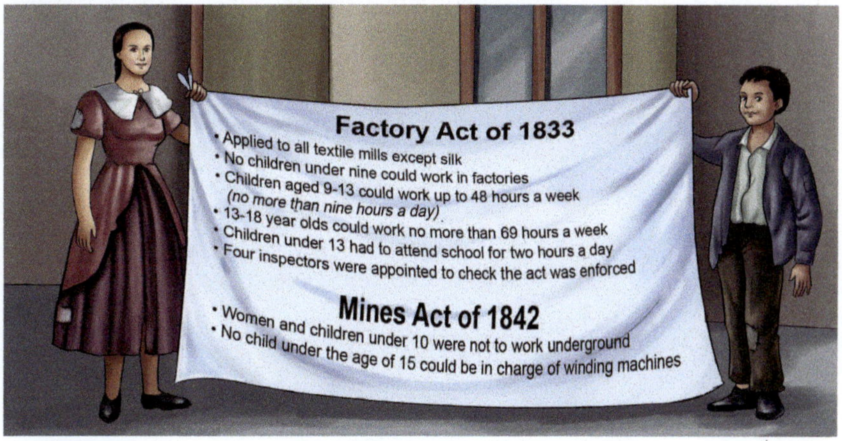

Problems with the acts?

Many workers did not support the factory reform acts as they limited the amount of money coming into a household. The acts did not cater for all workers and all factories. Furthermore, the reforms put poor people at a disadvantage and the existing poor relief did not support everyone. This led to the Poor Law Amendment Act of 1834. However, this law increased the pressure on workers: if they could not make enough money they were put into the dreaded workhouses. Families would be separated and lives ruined. Would life ever improve for the poor of Britain?

Work

1 What would each of the following think about factory reform:
   - a factory owner
   - a child worker who wants to go to school
   - a mother who has nine children to feed and little money
   - an upper-class lady who had read Lord Shaftsbury's report
   - a politician who believes in laissez-faire politics?

2 a Write two diary entries for a child in a factory. One should be from before 1833 and the other from after the factory reform act. You should try to show the good and bad consequences of the act.

   b Include a third entry about your little brother who was a trapper in the mines. Has his life changed after 1842?

8.3B Factory and social reform

The reform acts brought some improvements in working conditions. Mostly, they paved the way for further reform later in the nineteenth century, which reduced working hours, increased hours of education and made factories and mines safer. Who were the individuals – called **philanthropists** – behind reform, and why were they motivated by it?

Fact

Quakers are Protestants who believe in peaceful principles. They are **pacifists** and are committed to an equal society. This is why they were so heavily involved in social reform.

Name: Robert Owen and New Lanark

Famous quote: 'Eight hours labour, eight hours recreation, eight hours rest.'

Biography: Owen had run a successful mill in Manchester where he had treated his workers well. In 1800, he became manager and part-owner of his father-in-law's mill in Scotland. This was south of Glasgow and was called New Lanark.

Politics: He was a socialist: this meant he was not led so much by profits, but more about the wellbeing of his workers. He believed in a more equal society. Owen was also aware that happy workers would work better, and then he would have a better business.

Religion: He was not driven by religious motivations but did receive funding from a Quaker. Quakers were renowned for their desire to help the most vulnerable people in society.

What he changed: By 1810, he had introduced an eight-hour day (this was decades before the success of the 10-hour day campaign, which he was part of). He also opened a school in 1816 and all children had to have a certain number of hours of education, depending on their age. New Lanark had a social club and meeting areas for workers to visit in their time off. Drinking alcohol and swearing were banned in these places. New Lanark was visited by members of the royal family and MPs, and everyone agreed that it was a successful town.

Name: Edwin Chadwick

Famous quote: 'The formation of all habits of cleanliness is obstructed by defective supplies of water.'

Biography: Chadwick was from a **progressive** family and studied law at university. His father was a newspaper editor and was involved in progressive politics.

Politics: He made friends with people who were political philosophers; they were interested in social reform.

What he changed: He was responsible for the reform of the Poor Law that resulted in record numbers of people entering the workhouse in the 1830s; this made him very unpopular. However, he did write a report called 'The Sanitary Conditions of the Labouring Population'. This report showed that there was a link between the poor housing and sanitation of the factory workers and the outbreaks of killer diseases such as cholera. Most middle- and upper-class people had blamed the workers themselves.

Name: Elizabeth Fry

Biography: Fry was born to a Quaker family. Her mother helped various charities and her father was a well-respected Quaker who owned a factory.

Politics: She was a social reformer who believed in the poor being helped; she also believed in prison reform.

Religion: She was a strict Quaker.

Famous quote: 'Punishment is not for revenge but to lessen crime and reform the criminal.'

What she changed: She was shocked by the conditions she had heard of in Newgate Prison. In the prison she saw hundreds of women and children huddled on the floor in two cells. They had to sleep, cook and clean themselves in the cell. Children, there with their arrested mothers, sometimes had to share cells with murderers. Fry visited the prison regularly and soon established a school and a chapel. Her brother-in-law was an MP; he raised the issue of prison reform in parliament. As a result, prisons were reformed, as were the conditions for women on transportation ships.

Extension

GCSE

Research individuals such as George Cadbury, Titus Salt and Robert Peel Snr. What kind of reform did they engage in? What factors pushed them to become reformers? How much did they change things?

Practice Question

How far was religion the main factor that brought about improvements in the lives of working people in the nineteenth century?

16 marks

SPaG: 4 marks

Study Tip

Refer to individuals, governments and pressure groups. Use Chapters 7, 8 and 9 to help you with your answer.

Key Words

philanthropist pacifist progressive

Name: Josephine Butler

Biography: Butler was from a family of social reformers: her father was involved in the abolition of slavery.

Politics: She was a social reformer; her second cousin was Earl Grey.

Religion: She was an evangelical Christian.

Famous quote: 'It is unjust to punish the sex who are the victims of a vice, and leave unpunished the sex who are the main cause both of the vice and its dreaded consequences.'

What she changed: She was concerned with the issue of child prostitution, and campaigned for the age of consent to rise from 13 to 16. She was appalled by the way women were treated when they were arrested for being prostitutes. Society regarded these women as ungodly and unworthy of help. Butler saw their problems as poor wages, and men! In 1869, the Contagious Disease Act was introduced as a way of keeping sexually transmitted infections away from the armed forces. Any woman could be examined by a police officer if she was thought to be a prostitute. Butler's campaigning saw the repeal of the act in 1883.

Work

1. a What are the differences between factory reform and social reform?
   b Which one do you think made the biggest changes to people's lives?
2. a Elizabeth Fry's face is on a British £5 note. Explain why.
   b Do you think she deserves to be on the note more than the other reformers you have read about? Create a proposal in your groups to either keep Fry on the note or put another reformer on it.

9.1 The development of trade unionism: a new workers' paradise?

During the Industrial Revolution the working class grew in numbers. However, the relationship between factory owners and their workers was not always a good one. The workers often felt exploited by the factory owners, and sometimes grouped together to form trade unions. They felt that their working conditions were not good enough and the factory owners didn't look after the welfare of their workforce. Did the factory owners support the unions? Did trade unions make things better for the workers?

Objectives

- **Consider** the reasons people wanted trade unions.
- **Summarise** the key acts and movements in trade union history.
- **Analyse** the success of trade unions.

Workers' guilds

Since Medieval times there had been workers' **guilds** that controlled prices and wages. Before the Industrial Revolution businesses were small and the terms and conditions of service were negotiated person-to-person. Most business owners worked with their employees in small workshops so work was fair and conditions were good.

Once the Industrial Revolution took hold things changed. Work that had previously been done at home or in workshops was moved into factories. Wage competition was a massive problem, with immense increases in the working population. If someone had a grievance about their wages or working conditions they would simply be invited to leave, and someone else would be ready to take their job, often for a lower wage.

Opposition to new technology

There were many groups who fought against the changes in industry. The Luddites would deliberately break machinery in the hope that factory owners would turn away from technology. This did not have the desired effect.

▼ SOURCE A *A letter from 'Captain Swing', the fictional leader of the Swing Rioters; no one knows who actually wrote the letter, but it was probably an angry agricultural worker:*

> This is to inform you that if you don't pull down your machines and raise the wages of married men to two and six pence a day and single men to two shillings, we will burn down your barns and you in them. This is the last notice.

Another group, the Swing Rioters, were angered by the depression in agriculture after the Napoleonic wars, and by the new threshing machines that took their jobs. They set fire to farms and damaged the machines.

The Combination Act of 1825

There had been various combination acts since 1799. They put restrictions on groups of workers combining to form trade unions. After a wave of strikes in 1824, the Combination Act of 1825 was passed. This defined the rights of trade unions as meetings to discuss wages and conditions. Anything outside of this was illegal. The act was brought about to stop the perceived threat of intimidation by groups of workers. It also stopped them **picketing**. The problem with the act was that it was not clear about exactly what intimidation meant. However, the trade unions had been weakened.

Grand National Consolidated Trade Unions

Robert Owen, a mill owner in Scotland, was a keen supporter of workers' rights. He set up the Grand National Consolidated Trade Union (GNCTU) in 1834. This was to bring all workers together under one umbrella organisation.

Owen's cooperative movement saw the workers buying goods in bulk to sell on in their cooperative member shops. The profit from these shops was then shared among the working members.

Within a week of being set up the GNCTU had half a million members. The government was worried. However, the success of the GNCTU was short lived. The reality was that factory workers had different grievances from mine workers, and conflict between the two groups weakened the union. Its fate was sealed in 1834 when six farm labourers were arrested for swearing an oath to protect their income. Although union activity was not illegal, the swearing of an oath was.

In 1837, the Scottish Friendly Association of Cotton Spinners took **strike action**: when they were unhappy with something to do with their job, for example pay, they would refuse to work until their demands were met. They used violent methods, such as harassing people who were willing to work for less, and in extreme cases shooting them. Eventually, the spinners ran out of funds and their leaders were arrested. The strike ended in disaster.

New Model Unions

In 1851, a new type of union was set up: the Amalgamated Society of Engineers (ASE). This was a union of highly skilled men who could afford to pay weekly subscriptions: this would ensure they received sick pay and other benefits. Furthermore, if they threatened to strike their employer would suffer, as they could not replace them. This then sparked a wave of New Model Unions, with carpenters in 1860 and then tailors in 1866.

These New Model Unions were very successful, with the ASE boasting 33,000 members by 1868. The reason they were seen as 'new model' was because they were moderate in their outlook: they accepted the structure that they worked in, and did not want to destroy it. Rather, they wanted to negotiate improvement from within. This helped trade unionism gain support from the government. By the 1870s, trade unions had legal status and members could picket for their rights.

▶ **SOURCE B** *A trade union scroll from 1851 for the Amalgamated Society of Engineers, Machinists, Millwrights, Smiths and Pattern-Makers; this was presented to members when they joined*

Key Words

guild picket strike action

▼ **SOURCE C** *From a speech by William Allen, the General Secretary of the ASE, given in the 1850s:*

> The union does all it can to prevent any strike. We believe strikes to be a waste of money, not only in relation to the workers, but also to the employers.

New Unionism

The success of the New Model Unions had only benefited the more affluent skilled workers. There was a whole class of unskilled workers who were still unhappy. During the 1880s, this group organised themselves into action, and they had some success. The two most high-profile cases were the match girls' strike of 1888 and the dockers' strike of 1889. These strikes were successful: the trade union movement was strong.

This strength and order paved the way for a move into politics, with the creation of the Independent Labour Party; at the turn of the twentieth century this became the Labour Party we still have today. Trade unionism realised that it could best support and improve the lives of members by creating a political voice that could be heard.

Work

1. Write a definition for the following: New Model Union; workers' guilds; Luddites; GNCTU.
2. Write a list of all the reasons why someone would want to be a member of a trade union.
3. Draw a timeline of all the important events in trade union history.
4. Only the New Model Unions were a success. How far do you agree?

Practice Question

Explain the significance of New Model Unions for the development of workers' rights. **8 marks**

Study Tip

Refer to the influence of New Model Unions both at the time and during later trade union history.

9.2 The Tolpuddle Martyrs

The Industrial Revolution had brought new machines, new factories, new towns and new workers to the UK. Alongside this, workers had started to organise themselves into trade unions, to try to negotiate better pay and conditions. By 1834, unions were legal and growing in numbers. However, for six men in Dorset, union activity would result in them being put on a boat to Australia – and not for a holiday! Why, and how, were these people punished for being in a union? What were the consequences of this?

Objectives

- **Outline** the reasons why the Tolpuddle Martyrs were arrested.
- **Describe** why people were unhappy with their punishment.
- **Explain** the consequences of the Tolpuddle arrests.

Fact

This was a period when society moved from a focus on farming in the countryside and manufacturing on a small scale to a focus on machines, factories and industry in towns and cities. Large factories and large machines were built to do things people used to do by hand.

Who were the Tolpuddle Martyrs?

In a small village in Dorset called Tolpuddle, farm labourers had formed a union to try to negotiate better pay and conditions. The new farm machinery that had been invented meant fewer labourers were needed. Furthermore, anyone could operate the machines and no special training was needed, so wages dropped.

Being part of a trade union had been made legal so the men were not breaking any laws. They met under a sycamore tree in the village, or in a room in one of the members' cottages. Their leader was George Loveless. In February 1834, Loveless left for work and would not see his family again for years. He had been arrested.

The 'crime'

The men had not broken the law by being part of a trade union. However, part of the act to legalise unionism had stated that no secret oaths were to be taken. The men had all taken an oath to keep their union a secret, and so they had, in fact, broken this law.

The local landowner heard about this and was worried that the men had formed a union in the first place. Because of the French Revolution (a time when ordinary French citizens rebelled violently against their rulers), landowners and the government were scared that the ideas of equality and freedom would spread through Britain's working-class population. The Luddites and the Swing Rioters had not helped to ease their worries.

Luckily for the Tolpuddle landowner, and those in power who were also against trade unions, the six men could be arrested. The exact crime was, in a way, irrelevant. The message to the working class was clear – no unions!

▼ **SOURCE A** *A poster warning that people found guilty of uttering illegal oaths and joining unions would be transported; this was put up in Dorset in February 1834*

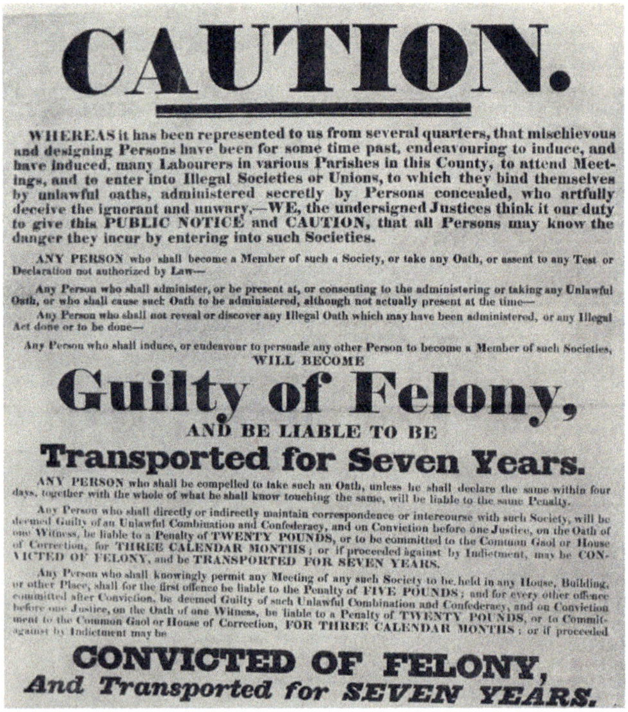

CAUTION.

WHEREAS it has been represented to us from several quarters, that mischievous and designing Persons have been for some time past, endeavouring to induce, and have induced, many Labourers in various Parishes in this County, to attend Meetings, and to enter into Illegal Societies or Unions, to which they bind themselves by unlawful oaths, administered secretly by Persons concealed, who artfully deceive the ignorant and unwary,—WE, the undersigned Justices think it our duty to give this PUBLIC NOTICE and CAUTION, that all Persons may know the danger they incur by entering into such Societies.

ANY PERSON who shall become a Member of such a Society, or take any Oath, or assent to any Test or Declaration not authorized by Law—

Any Person who shall administer, or be present at, or consenting to the administering or taking any Unlawful Oath, or who shall cause such Oath to be administered, although not actually present at the time—

Any Person who shall not reveal or discover any Illegal Oath which may have been administered, or any Illegal Act done or to be done—

Any Person who shall induce, or endeavour to persuade any other Person to become a Member of such Societies, WILL BECOME

Guilty of Felony,

AND BE LIABLE TO BE

Transported for Seven Years.

ANY PERSON who shall be compelled to take such an Oath, unless he shall declare the same within four days, together with the whole of what he shall know touching the same, will be liable to the same Penalty.

Any Person who shall directly or indirectly maintain correspondence or intercourse with such Society, will be deemed Guilty of an Unlawful Combination and Confederacy, and on Conviction before one Justice, on the Oath of one Witness, be liable to a Penalty of TWENTY POUNDS, or to be committed to the Common Gaol or House of Correction, for THREE CALENDAR MONTHS; or if proceeded against by Indictment, may be CONVICTED OF FELONY, and be TRANSPORTED FOR SEVEN YEARS.

Any Person who shall knowingly permit any Meeting of any such Society to be held in any House, Building, or other Place, shall for the first offence be liable to the Penalty of FIVE POUNDS; and for every other offence committed after Conviction, be deemed Guilty of such Unlawful Combination and Confederacy, and on Conviction before one Justice, on the Oath of one Witness, be liable to a Penalty of TWENTY POUNDS, or to Commitment to the Common Gaol or House of Correction, FOR THREE CALENDAR MONTHS; or if proceeded against by Indictment may be

CONVICTED OF FELONY,
And Transported for SEVEN YEARS.

The punishment

The men were found guilty of making an unlawful oath, and were sentenced to seven years' transportation to Australia. There they would endure hard labour.

Public reaction and consequences

Word spread quickly about the sentences the men had received. Soon there were various organisations and groups who were committed to overturning the decision made about the group, now named the Tolpuddle Martyrs. Robert Owen called a meeting of the GNCTU; 10,000 people arrived to attend.

The march at Copenhagen Fields was attended by thousands of working-class supporters, and many prominent individuals such as William Cobbett and Robert Owen. The supporters gathered petitions and demanded that the Tolpuddle Martyrs be returned to England.

The government was originally reluctant to reverse the decision made, but eventually the persistent campaigning paid off. On 14 March 1836, all six of the men were given a full and free pardon. The trade unions had won.

Many of the people involved in the movement to free the Tolpuddle Martyrs also got involved in Chartism and cooperative societies, as a way to make the lives of all working ordinary people better.

▼ **SOURCE C** *A drawing of the demonstration in support of the Tolpuddle Martyrs, held at Copenhagen Fields in London on 21 April 1834*

▼ **B** *Maps showing where the six Tolpuddle Martyrs went to in Australia*

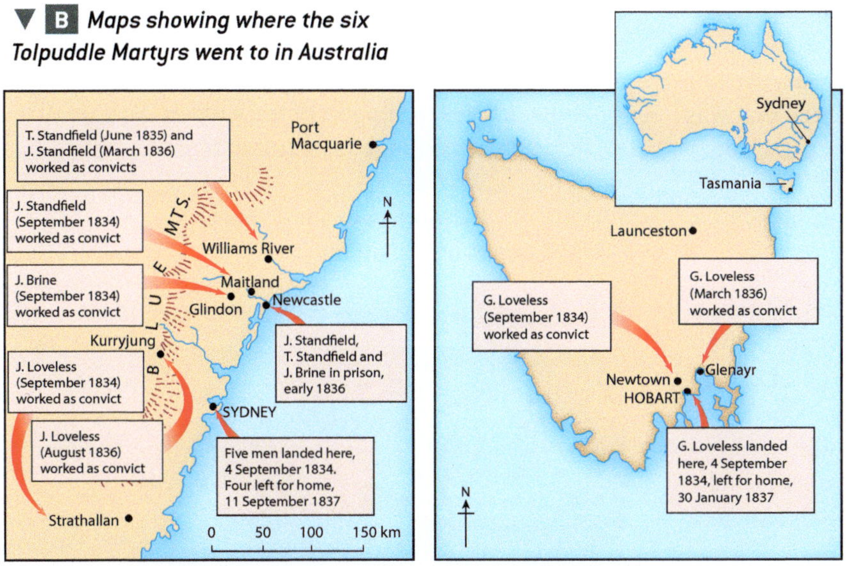

Work

1. **a** Write as many reasons as you can to explain why the Tolpuddle Martyrs were arrested.
   b Next to each reason provide a statement about why this would upset the government.
   c Now write another statement saying why it was important for the workers.
2. Why would people be upset that the Tolpuddle Martyrs had been transported? Use the map showing the work they did, and think about the workers who were left in Britain.
3. Why did many people who campaigned for the Tolpuddle Martyrs go on to join Chartism? How similar were the movements?
4. Create the table below in your book. Complete it for the Topuddle Martyrs, then go back to look at the trade unions on the previous pages, and add to the table. Leave room so you can add to it when you look at other working-class unions.

	Date	Successful?	Not successful?	Sources to support?
Tolpuddle Martyrs				

Extension

Find out what happened to all the Topuddle Martyrs after they were pardoned.

9.3 New Unionism: how successful were working-class unions?

In the 1850s, the New Model Unions made life better for specialised, highly skilled workers, such as engineers and carpenters. However, unskilled workers still had difficulty organising themselves to improve their conditions. The growth of New Unionism, as it was called, was spurred on by two strikes in the 1880s. This New Unionism would ensure the voices of the unskilled working class were heard; things were about to change. What tactics did New Unionism use? How successful were they?

Objectives

- **Compare** the causes of the strikes in the 1880s.
- **Explain** why the strikes were successful.
- **Assess** evidence to analyse how successful working-class unions were.

Why did matchbox factory workers go on strike?

One of the most prominent factories making matches was the Bryant & May factory in London. It employed women to make the matches, many of them young girls. The conditions in the factory were poor and many of the girls and women working there became very ill; some even died. The most common illness was 'phossy jaw'. This was caused by the white phosphorus that was used to make the matches light. The chemical caused their jaws to rot, meaning their teeth fell out. Those who survived the illness were left with disfigured faces.

If that wasn't enough, the workers were paid poor wages: around 20 pence a week for a girl and 40 pence for a woman. They were often fined at the whim of the factory owner, for not working fast enough or for being late to work, for example. In 1882, money was deducted from their wages to fund a new statue of Prime Minister William Gladstone. The women had had enough, and in July 1888 they decided to go on strike.

Strike action and support

A journalist, Annie Besant, had become aware of the conditions the women worked in. She helped to organise the strike action, and supported the workers. The strike quickly caught the imagination and sympathy of the general public. Here were young women, being paid little for hard and dangerous work.

Besant organised the grievances of the women in a publication: 'White Slaves of London'. With it she called for a boycott of the matches made at Bryant & May. The factory owners put pressure on the women who were not striking to deny the claims made by Besant. When one refused she was dismissed from her job. As a result, a further 1400 workers came out in support of the strike, during which Besant:

- asked for higher wages for the women and registered them for strike pay
- wrote articles in support of the women
- held public meetings to raise awareness of the match factory conditions
- marched the women in a procession to the Houses of Parliament.

▼ **SOURCE A** *Workers from the match factory, 1888*

Lucky strike!

All of the strike action paid off. The employers agreed to the demands and removed the system of deductions and fines. The matchbox workers were also given a pay rise. This was the first successful strike by unskilled manual workers.

The dockers' strike

A year after the match girls' strike, the London dockers went on strike, demanding better pay and working conditions. They were also inspired by the successful gas workers' strike. The dockers were striking for a wage rise, from five pence an hour to six pence (the 'docker's tanner'). They also wanted eight pence an hour for any overtime work. The dockers had the added problem of having to compete for work. They would regularly go days without work – just turning up in the morning to see if they were needed. They needed to change this and wanted to secure at least four hours a day.

Tactics of the dockers

The New Unionism strikes were more **militant** than the actions of the New Model Unions, mostly because the New Unionism leaders were socialists. The dockers' leader was Ben Tillet; he was adamant the men should get better working conditions. He encouraged them to march through London to raise the profile of the strike and get support. The men carried rotten vegetables and fish heads to show the public what they and their families were living on.

The men also picketed the gates of London docks. This way they could continue to put pressure on the managers and stop any 'blackleg' labourers entering the docks to do the work. This was certainly a move away from the negotiations of the Amalgamated Society of Engineers.

Did the dockers get their tanner?

The strike action closed London docks and gained the support of some influential people, including the Lord Mayor of London and Cardinal Manning, who mediated between the dock owners and the workers. The public, as with the match girls, were sympathetic to the dockers' plight and supported their demands. A generous donation of £30,000 from unions in Australia helped support the strike action. This forced the hand of the dock owners and the men received their pay rise and a guaranteed four-hour day.

The success of the match girls' strike and the dockers' strike was an important milestone in union history. Union membership increased and unskilled workers now had a voice. Did this pave the way for other groups in society to find their voices?

Key Word

militant

▼ **SOURCE B** *A poster appealing for donors to the striking dockers' relief fund*

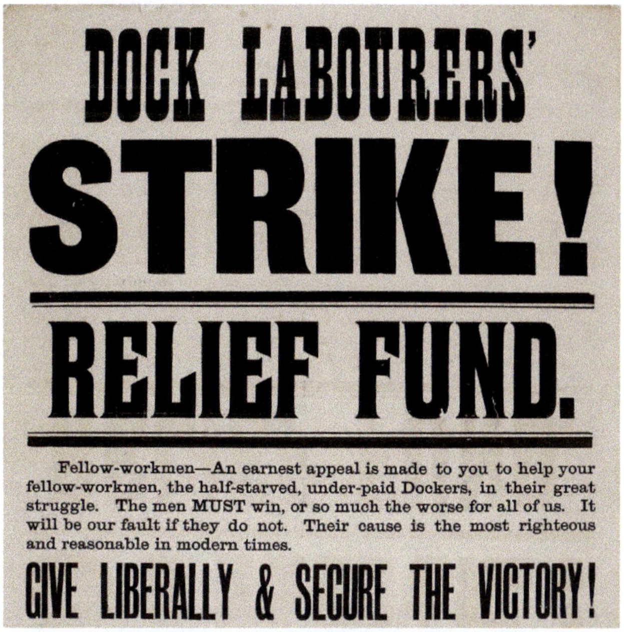

Work

1. List the similarities and the differences of the two strikes.
2. What lessons do you think workers in other industries learned from the match girls' strike?
3. Complete the table you started on the Tolpuddle Martyrs. Pick out the successes and find a source that supports your point.
4. Use the table to answer the question: How successful were working-class unions? Try to show both sides of the argument.

Practice Question

Explain two ways in which Chartism and New Unionism were similar. **8 marks**

Study Tip

It would be easy to confuse New Model Unions and New Unionism, so make sure you know exactly what you are comparing! Think about the kind of people who were involved, and the outcomes of the movements.

10.1 Where was a woman's place?

By 1913, the suffragette movement was in full swing. The Prime Minister had been attacked, buildings had been burned down, some women were starving themselves to death and others had been arrested. One suffragette even died after being hit by a horse during the world famous Derby horse race. Why did such a violent movement emerge, just for the vote? How did the government react? Did the violent methods work?

Objectives

- **Identify** attitudes to women in the nineteenth century.
- **Describe** why women wanted the vote.
- **Predict** which group would have the most success.

A woman's place?

During the Industrial Revolution, women had started to work in factories and to earn more money than they ever had working from home. There were many reforms that improved the working conditions for women in factories and mines. For middle-class women, however, their world still revolved around the home. In addition, many people believe that the reforms for the working class were actually an attempt to put women back in the home, where they could look after their husbands and children.

There were some acts during the nineteenth century that made life better for women, such as the Married Women's Property Act, 1870. This allowed women to control their own income and property after marriage. Previously, their income and property had been under the control of their husbands. This had meant women were dependent on men, but the new act started to change this.

Despite the changes, women had certainly not achieved equality by the start of the twentieth century. Most professions expected women to leave when they got married: their job was now to be a wife and a mother. Even if women did the same jobs as men they were paid less. As was the case for many groups before, the one way to bring about change would be for women to have representation in government. Women needed the vote!

Millicent Fawcett and the National Union of Women's Suffrage Societies

The need to persuade men that women deserved the vote became organised in 1897. By this time women had been able to vote in local elections and school board elections. However, for real change, women would need to be able to vote at a national level.

Millicent Fawcett, the wife of the **Liberal** MP Henry Fawcett, brought all the groups campaigning for women's suffrage together to form the National Union of Women's Suffrage Societies (NUWSS). They became known as the Suffragists. This was a collection of middle-class women who believed in using peaceful methods, such as meetings, speeches, posters and letters, to achieve the vote.

The Pankhursts and the Women's Social and Political Union

Some Suffragists became frustrated with how long it was taking for change to occur. In 1903, a member of the Manchester branch of the NUWSS – Emmeline Pankhurst – decided that it was time to take more direct action.

▼ **SOURCE A** *An NUWSS poster showing the root of the campaign and the different branches that made up the NUWSS*

▼ **SOURCE B** *Millicent Fawcett, pictured around 1890*

Mrs Pankhurst and her two daughters, Sylvia and Christabel, formed the Women's Social and Political Union (WSPU). They believed in 'deeds not words' and were not scared to live up to their motto.

The Pankhursts were middle class and had a long history of supporting women's causes. Emmeline's husband had been Richard Pankhurst. He was a lawyer who had written the Married Women's Property Act.

The Women's Freedom League

By 1907, the WSPU had many members who engaged in the militant tactics promoted by the Pankhursts and other leaders. However, there were many who wanted change but did not believe in violent methods. They were mostly pacifists. These women broke away and created the Women's Freedom League (WFL). As well as campaigning for the vote, they also campaigned for equal pay for women. There were now three different groups, all campaigning for the same cause. They all wanted the vote; they just had different ways of campaigning for it.

▼ **SOURCE C** ***Emmeline Pankhurst; born in 1858, she founded the Women's Franchise League in 1889. This fought to allow married women to vote in local elections.***

Extension

GCSE

The idea of equality for women was not a new concept by the twentieth century. Research the work of Mary Wollstonecraft. Why do you think nothing changed for women when she was writing in the eighteenth century? What else was happening in the world that might have led Wollstonecraft to believe change was possible?

Key Words

liberal

▶ **SOURCE D** ***An original WSPU rosette; the colours used were for specific reasons – purple signified dignity, green showed hope and white symbolised purity***

▼ **SOURCE E** ***Sophia Duleep Singh, from an Indian royal family and a goddaughter of Queen Victoria, was an active member of the WSPU. She often sold*** **The Suffragette** ***near her home in Richmond.***

Work

1. Copy out the following statements about women in the nineteenth century. Next to them write TRUE or FALSE:
   - Women could vote in national elections.
   - A woman was expected to leave her job when she got married.
   - A woman's husband would legally own all her money and property on marriage.
   - A woman was paid less than a man for doing the same job.
2. Explain what Millicent Fawcett, Emmeline Pankhurst and a member of the Women's Freedom League would agree and disagree about, concerning women's suffrage.
3. Which group do you think would have had the most success? Write a letter to the leader explaining why you would like to join them.

10.2A What was the impact of the campaign for women's suffrage?

By 1914, the campaign for women's suffrage had gathered pace; it now had many supporters. The women were developing their tactics and gaining support. However, the First World War caused a change in the role of women. Did it help with their campaign? Which branch of the movement gained most support and which had the most success? Did women get the vote?

Objectives

- **Describe** the different tactics used in the campaign for the vote for women.
- **Explain** the government response to the suffragettes' actions.
- **Evaluate** the success of the violent tactics used in the campaign.

Give peace a chance

The NUWSS used their political contacts to lobby MPs. They pledged to support MPs who believed in universal suffrage. Their members were trained to speak publicly, in a persuasive but non-violent way. They created petitions and pamphlets to persuade the nation and those in government that women deserved the vote. Many people were persuaded by the campaign, but some members felt that the Suffragists' actions were too easy to ignore.

Despite their placid tactics, the NUWSS did have many supporters throughout the early twentieth century. When the government did not pass an act in 1912 to extend the vote to women, the NUWSS started a pilgrimage from Carlisle to London. Thousands of people joined the march in support.

We need change now!

Led by Emmeline Pankhurst, some WSPU members decided to use more militant tactics. They were prepared to use more extreme, often violent methods. They were referred to as suffragettes, to distinguish them from the Suffragists. To begin with, they had the support of the Liberal Prime Minister, Henry Campbell-Bannerman, who told the women to pester the government and not to show patience.

Their tactics included heckling members of parliament during speeches. They stood outside the House of Commons and held demonstrations. In 1912, they started a stone-throwing campaign. Hundreds of windows were smashed and over 200 suffragettes were arrested. This was all part of their plan: the court cases got them extra publicity.

The suffragettes took their actions further, making arson attacks and blowing up buildings. MPs were put on high alert. They were warned to be suspicious of parcels in case they contained explosives. In 1913, parliament made another attempt to give women the vote. This failed.

Derby Day, 1913

At the Derby horse race at Epsom in 1913, the king's horse was running round the racecourse when it was brought to the ground by a woman who had deliberately walked onto the racecourse as the horses approached. This woman was Emily Wilding Davison, and she died of her wounds in hospital, soon after the incident. She was a suffragette, and became the first **martyr** of the suffrage movement. Historians are divided about whether Davison had planned to kill herself that day. It seems she might have been trying to stick a suffragette rosette on the horse, but she was trampled as the horse was going too fast. There is uncertainty about her intentions and whether she meant to kill herself because she had bought herself a return ticket home.

▼ **SOURCE A** ***A portrait of Sir Thomas Carlyle that was slashed by a suffragette; the way she slashed the face made people worry that suffragettes may do this in real life***

Key Word

martyr

Regardless, the movement now had evidence of how committed their members were. They were so serious about getting the vote that they were willing to die for it. Emily Davison was given a headstone that said: Deeds not words.

▼ **SOURCE B** *The cover of* The Suffragette *magazine, 13 June 1913*

Why does the cat chase the mouse?

The suffragette tactics extended to their time in prison. They were often arrested for their violent attacks, or for disturbing the peace by chaining themselves to railings. When they were in prison, many went on hunger strike. This is a tactic used by prisoners as a way to continue their campaign by gaining publicity. The government knew they could not have women dying in prison: these women were middle-class, and many had husbands or fathers who held influential jobs. Prison officers initially tried force-feeding the suffragettes. However, this was dangerous and could lead to disabilities and death.

Due to the dangers of force-feeding, the government passed the Prisoners (Temporary Discharge for Ill Health) Act in 1913. This would allow them to release the women when they became too weak from starvation. Once they had been rehabilitated and were healthy enough to return to prison, they would be re-arrested. The act thus became known as the 'Cat and Mouse Act'.

▼ **SOURCE C** ***Adapted from an account of a suffragette on hunger strike; the WSPU were able to publish her account in a pamphlet while she was still in prison before the 'Cat and Mouse Act':***

> I was then surrounded and forced back onto the chair, which was tilted backwards. There were about ten persons around me. The doctor then forced my mouth so as to form a pouch, and held me while one of the wardresses poured some liquid from a spoon; it was milk and brandy. While I was held down a nasal tube was inserted. It is two yards long, with a funnel at the end; there is a glass junction in the middle to see if the liquid is passing. Great pain is experienced during the process, both mental and physical.

► **SOURCE D** *A suffragette poster about the 'Cat and Mouse Act', showing a cat (representing the police, the prison authorities and the government) holding a mouse (representing a suffragette) in its mouth. Many people were against this act, which seemed to prolong the suffering of women by repeatedly re-arresting them, and public sympathy for the suffragette movement grew as a result.*

Work

1. Write out as many tactics as you can that the different groups used. Colour code them to show which would have a long-term impact and which would have a short-term impact.
2. **a** What tactics do **Sources A**, **B** and **C** tell you about?
   b Why is Davison portrayed as an angel in **Source B**?
   c Do you think this would convince people to support the suffragettes?
   d Which one of the sources gives details of the most effective tactic, in your opinion?
3. Why did the government introduce the 'Cat and Mouse Act'?
4. Look at **Source D**. Create your own propaganda poster that shows a tactic and the response it got. You can create the poster from the government's or the WSPU's perspective.
5. How useful is **Source B** to a historian researching suffragette tactics?

10.2B What was the impact of the campaign for women's suffrage?

Responses to militancy

The suffragettes were starting to gain criticism for their actions, with many people at the time feeling that they were actually preventing women getting the vote, rather than helping. Their violent actions made them look, in some people's eyes, irrational and unbalanced. These were exactly the reasons that many people had used to not give women the vote.

▼ **INTERPRETATION E** *Adapted from* The Place of Women: 1700 to the Present Day *(1971), written by John Ray:*

> The opposition was great. Some men objected to women having the vote because they believed them to be inferior. It was suggested that women could not think out matters coolly and calmly. Others would not agree to women's suffrage because they did not want change. Women had never voted before. Why should they start now? A further objection involved property. In 1900, few women were householders or lodgers. If the vote were given to them, then it would have to be given also to men who were not householders or lodgers. At that time political parties were not prepared to do this.

▶ **SOURCE F**

A poster, produced by the National League for Opposing Woman Suffrage, called 'A Suffragette's Home'; the note stuck on the poster says, 'Back in an hour or so'

Even many women objected to the campaign for universal suffrage. These women believed a woman's place was at home, supporting her husband and caring for her children. They did not think politics was a world women belonged in. This was a view held by the Liberal Prime Minister, Herbert Asquith. Asquith did not support votes for women; he believed the decision should only be made if it improved government and the political process. He could see no argument for why it would and therefore opposed extending the franchise to women.

The angel of the factory

When war broke out in 1914, the NUWSS and WPSU united to support the war effort. The suffragettes stopped their militant and violent campaign, and as a result of the work they did they earned themselves the nickname of 'angel of the factory'. The Women's Freedom League, however, refused to support the war effort. As pacifists, they did not want to support the men fighting in Europe.

It is widely accepted by historians that women's war work helped them get the vote. They worked in factories, on farms and even at the front line, as nurses. This showed that women could do the same jobs as men. It also proved that women could make clear-headed decisions, not only in factories but in running family businesses and driving ambulances in dangerous circumstances at the front line. Lastly, the argument that women were not as intelligent was contradicted by the fact they managed to successfully look after the family, run the home and do the jobs their husbands had done. Women proved they could do it all.

The post-war situation

After the war, the men who returned from the trenches moved back into their jobs. Many women moved back into the home. Before the outbreak of war, the government had accepted that some women should have the vote. The government also had to consider that a lot of the men who had gone to fight did not have the vote: this was recognised as unfair. Thus, in 1918 the Representation of the People Act was passed. This gave all men over the age of 21 the vote, and some women over the age of 21, if they owned property, otherwise they had to be over 30. This was a success for the wealthy middle-class women but did nothing for working-class women. Some women continued to campaign until, in 1928, women were given the vote on equal terms with men.

Women throughout the twentieth century

The campaign for women's rights did not stop in 1928. In the 1960s, a new movement developed in Britain and the USA. This was the Women's Movement. Women were no longer campaigning for the vote but for a different kind of equality. They wanted equal pay with men, increased numbers of women in higher education, 24-hour child care, free contraception and abortion on demand. They wanted women to have the same rights and freedoms as men. The movement was successful, with the government passing the Divorce Reform Act in 1969, arguably an extension of the Married Woman's Property Act. The 1969 act allowed women to divorce their husbands easily, and they were entitled to claim any property owned in the divorce settlement. In 1970 the Equal Pay Act and in 1975 the Sex Discrimination Act gave women more rights and protection in the workplace. This was all happening during a time of social change: the government of Harold Wilson was creating a more liberal society. Not only were women's lives changed: Wilson also changed the law so that homosexuality was no longer illegal; he tried to end discrimination against ethnic minorities; and he abolished capital punishment.

There remains today a wage gap between men and women in Britain. Women are still not completely equal with men, but the suffragettes ensured that women could do something to change it. They could vote and be part of the political process.

▼ **SOURCE G** *Women marching in New York to commemorate the fiftieth anniversary of women's suffrage in the USA, August 1970*

Work

1. Give three reasons against universal suffrage that were used before 1914.
2. Why do you think women did not get the vote before 1914?
3. **a** Create a timeline showing all the key acts/events in the journey for women's suffrage. Which events were indirect reasons why women got the vote? Which was the spark?
   b Make your timeline a 'concept timeline' by showing periods of tension and good relations between the government and the suffragettes.
4. 'Women's war work got them the vote.' How far do you agree? You need to compare their war work with their militant tactics. Which one had the biggest impact?
5. How do you think Emmeline Pankhurst would feel if she could see **Source G**?

Extension

GCSE

Research the impact of the following: the New English Law of Property (1926), the Law Reform Act (1935), the Education Act (1944), the Abortion Act (1967), the Equal Pay Act (1970), the Employment Protection Act (1975), and the publication of *The Female Eunuch* (1969) and *Spare Rib* (July 1972).

Practice Question

Explain two ways in which the Chartist campaign and the campaign for women's suffrage were similar.

8 marks

Study Tip

Explore the split in both groups – they both had peaceful and militant branches. Both had clear leaders as well: did their leadership help or hinder the success of each movement?

11.1A The General Strike, 1926

In May 1926, Britain was almost at a standstill. Coal miners across the country were angered by falling wages and increased working hours: they decide to go on strike. Britain faced the prospect of no transport, coal or electricity. In order to prevent disaster the Conservative government had to act quickly. In the end, the General Strike lasted for nine days, with workers from heavy industries such as the steel industry, shipbuilding and the railway industry supporting the striking miners. Did the strike result in better working conditions for the miners? Did the government and unions work together to resolve the issues?

Objectives

- **Explain** the causes of the General Strike of 1926.
- **Analyse** the causes and consequences of the strike.
- **Evaluate** evidence using your own knowledge.

Britain after the First World War

During the First World War, because of the demand for armaments, Britain's heavy industries enjoyed high output and a dramatic increase in people working for them. All coal mines had been **nationalised** during the war, and the miners had hoped that they would be continue to be owned by the country when war ended. This would mean the government would be obliged to invest money, thus their jobs would be safe. However, after the war the government was quick to return control of the mines to their private owners.

After 1918, the future was not looking good for Britain's mining industry, as there was a fall in the demand for coal. So, the mine owners needed to dramatically reduce costs: their mines had to become more efficient in order to make money. One option the owners had was to close down mines that were inefficient: this meant they could concentrate production on the mines that were making the most money. Another option was to start introducing new automatic machinery: this meant fewer men were needed as the machines could do a lot of the work, a situation similar to the one at the start of the Industrial Revolution.

A *Bar graphs showing the output of coal in the UK and the USA in 1913 and 1920*

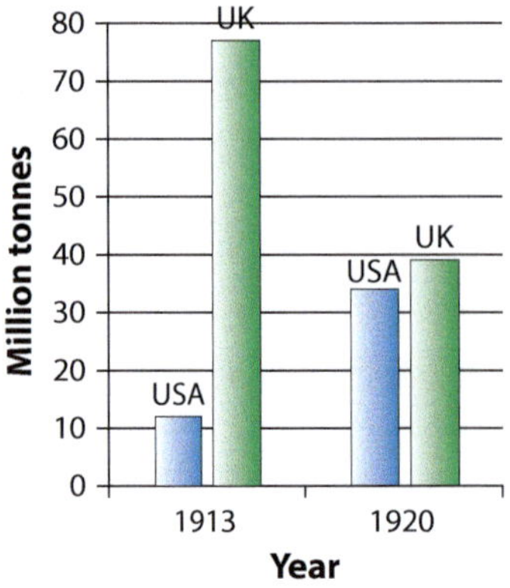

British mines were the pits

Foreign competition and a lack of modern technology pushed British coal mine owners further into crisis. Mines in countries such as Germany had more modern equipment, as they were owned by big companies that could invest lots of money in new technology. Increasingly, British mines could not compete with their output. The unions wanted the government to **re-nationalise** the mines; the mines needed investment.

INTERPRETATION B *Adapted from* British Economic and Social History, *1987, written by modern historian Philip Sauvain:*

> [By the early 1920s] Poland and Germany, as well as the United States, were challenging Britain's supremacy in the export of coal. Their coal was easier to mine. They had lower labour costs and often lower transport costs as well.

Black Friday

On Friday 15 April 1921, mine owners announced an extension of the working day, along with a drop in wages. The miners were outraged and decided to strike. Worried that other employers would do the same as the mine owners, the Trades Union Congress (TUC) called other industries out on strike in **solidarity**. However, at the last minute the railway and dockers' unions pulled out. They did not feel the immediate concerns as the miners did; they were not as worried for their jobs. And so, left alone without any support from other industries, the miners felt that they had no other option but to return to work with longer days and for lower wages.

Red Friday

In 1925, the price of coal fell again and the mine owners declared further changes to hours and pay. Prime Minister Stanley Baldwin knew that the other unions would support the miners this time. He was worried about a workers' revolution and knew he had to do something to stop the unrest. On Friday 31 July 1925, Baldwin agreed to subsidise the coal industry. He also set up the Samuels Commission, the job of which was to reach an agreement between the miners and the mine owners. Many people believed that Baldwin was just buying time with the commission, so he could prepare Britain for the inevitable General Strike. But the miners were happy, for now.

Workers, unite!

In April 1926, Baldwin's subsidy money ran out: the TUC met to discuss action. On 1 May – May Day: a day when workers' rights are celebrated – they agreed to strike. On 3 May, Britain's first General Strike began: ships sat unloaded in docks, trains didn't move and coal wasn't mined. The strike divided the country.

Fact

Friday 15 April is known as Black Friday because many workers felt betrayed by their union leaders. Friday 31 July is known as Red Friday because the workers achieved a victory with the government subsidies.

▶ **SOURCE C** *A cartoon shown in a trade union magazine in 1925; it is called 'The Subsidised Mineowner – Poor Beggar!'*

THE SUBSIDISED MINEOWNER—POOR BEGGAR!

Key Words

nationalise foreign competition re-nationalise solidarity

▼ **SOURCE D** *Arthur James Cook, a trade union leader, addressing miners in October 1929*

Work

1 Why had Britain's heavy industries enjoyed a boom period before 1921?

2 a Create a mind-map showing the causes of the General Strike in 1926. You should annotate it with detail from the text and the sources. Try to categorise the causes.

b Can you justify why one cause was more important than the other?

3 a What information about the General Strike can you infer from **Source C**?

b Which side is being represented in **Source C**? Explain your answer using the source and your own knowledge.

c Is **Source C** a good source for researching the causes of the General Strike?

Extension

Research the issues that lead to large numbers of workers going on strike in Britain today.

11.1B The General Strike, 1926

The nine days

The General Strike lasted for nine days in May 1926. The table below shows the actions taken by each side to either make the strike effective or try to limit its impact.

▼ **E** *Government and TUC actions*

Government actions:	TUC actions:
Used the Emergency Powers Act from the First World War to arrange for the army to take over the jobs of the striking workers.	Created their own newspaper, *The British Worker*, and used it to explain the motivations for the strike.
Encouraged middle-class students to take a break from university and work in heavy industries; more than 226,000 student volunteers did this.	Also used the paper to remind strikers to remain peaceful and not use violent tactics.
Started a propaganda campaign with their own newspaper, *The British Gazette*, which tried to turn the public against the strikers; the newspaper was edited by Winston Churchill.	Some strikers did become violent and there were clashes with the police.
Stanley Baldwin made speeches referring to the strike as a revolution; this fuelled the public's fear of **communism**.	Strikers travelled the country to picket with other industries in solidarity.
Armoured cars, driven by the army and police, were sent to key cities to stop the violent clashes between the strikers and government supporters. They were armed with machine guns.	Funds were set up to help feed the strikers and their families. This would ensure the strike could keep going.

▼ **SOURCE F** *The front page of* The British Gazette, *5 May 1926; this was the government newspaper*

The British Gazette
Published by His Majesty's Stationery Office.

FIRST DAY OF GREAT STRIKE

Not So Complete as Hoped by its Promoters

PREMIER'S AUDIENCE OF THE KING

Miners and the General Council Meet at House of Commons

FOOD SUPPLIES

HOLD-UP OF THE NATION

Government and the Challenge

COMMUNIST LEADER ARRESTED

THE "BRITISH GAZETTE" AND ITS OBJECTS

Reply to Strike Makers' Plan to Paralyse Public Opinion

REAL MEANING OF THE STRIKE

Conflict Between Trade Union Leaders and Parliament

▼ **SOURCE G** *The front page of* The British Worker, *13 May 1926; this was the official strike news bulletin*

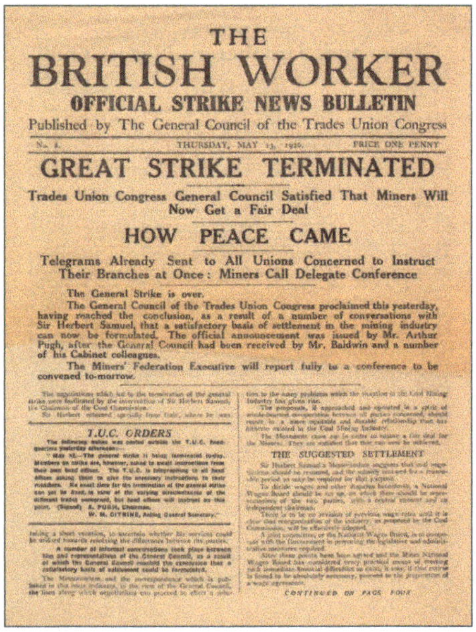
THE BRITISH WORKER

OFFICIAL STRIKE NEWS BULLETIN

Published by The General Council of the Trades Union Congress

THURSDAY, MAY 13, 1926. PRICE ONE PENNY

GREAT STRIKE TERMINATED

Trades Union Congress General Council Satisfied That Miners Will Now Get a Fair Deal

HOW PEACE CAME

Telegrams Already Sent to All Unions Concerned to Instruct Their Branches at Once: Miners Call Delegate Conference

The General Strike is over.

The General Council of the Trades Union Congress proclaimed this yesterday, having reached the conclusion, as a result of a number of conversations with Sir Herbert Samuel, that a satisfactory basis of settlement in the mining industry can now be formulated. The official announcement was issued by Mr. Arthur Pugh, after the General Council had been received by Mr. Baldwin and a number of his Cabinet colleagues.

The Miners' Federation Executive will report fully to a conference to be convened to-morrow.

T.U.C. ORDERS

THE SUGGESTED SETTLEMENT

◀ **SOURCE H**
A volunteer worker helping a railway passenger during the strike in 1926

Back to work

After nine days, on 12 May, the strike ended with the TUC deciding to negotiate with the government and finally accepting the findings of the Samuel Commission. The miners' federation had refused to take part in these negotiations. Some slight changes made to Samuel's report were enough for the TUC leaders, and they encouraged the miners to return to work. By this time, the TUC had run out of money and could not possibly continue with the strike action. They had been defeated by the government who had been preparing for the strike for nine months; it had been paying the subsidy to the mine owners. Furthermore, the violent actions of some meant that public opinion had gone against the strikers. Moreover, the party that was meant to represent the workers, the Labour Party, was not in full support of the strike action. Workers in all industries, apart from the miners, returned to work. The miners did not fully return to work until November, when they were forced back by hunger and disillusionment. They worked longer hours for lower wages: many felt that the strike had been for nothing.

Consequences of the strike for the unions

After the failure of the General Strike, union membership fell dramatically. This coincided with a rise in unemployment. The government passed the Trade Disputes and Trade Unions Act in 1927, which made it illegal for unions to join together to strike. Unions could no longer use money from union memberships to fund political parties: all members had to agree for this to happen. This had an impact on the unions' relationship with the Labour Party and weakened the power of the unions. Union membership would not reach peak levels again until the Second World War.

▼ **SOURCE I** *A* Punch *cartoon from 1926 showing the constitutional government and the TUC lever breaking under it; this showed the weakness of the TUC*

Key Word

communism

Work

1. a. Describe three tactics used by each side during the General Strike.
   b. Explain why the tactics were used. Can you say which was the most effective?
2. What can you learn from **Source I** about why the strike failed?
3. a. Work with a partner. One of you should write an article for *The British Gazette*, outlining the causes and events of the General Strike. The other person should write an article for *The British Worker*. Your articles should be no longer than 200 words.
   b. In what ways are your articles similar?
   c. In what ways are they different?
   d. Can you suggest reasons why they are different?

Practice Question

How useful is **Source I** to a historian studying the General Strike and the reasons for its failure?

8 marks

Study Tip

Remember that sources can have clear opinions about the General Strike. You have to be able to explain why it has this view and if this makes it more or less useful. You should try to refer to the source being one-sided; this way you will always consider the other side.

Extension

GCSE

The left-wing historian A. J. P. Taylor has written lots about the twentieth century, with a focus on the Second World War. His politics mean that he supported workers' revolutions; but he was also a pacifist. He stated, 'The strikers asked nothing for themselves. They did not seek to challenge the government but still less to overthrow the constitution. They merely wanted the miners to have a living wage. They were loyal to their unions, as they had been loyal during the war to their country and their generals. They once more went into the trenches, without enthusiasm and with little hope.' How has Taylor presented the strikers? Why does he have this interpretation?

11.2 Trade union reform

In 1900, only 12 per cent of Britain's labour force had been in a trade union. By 1984, the proportion had grown to around 50 per cent. One of the key tactics available to workers in a trade union is to go on strike if they are unhappy about something relating to their job. By the 1980s, British workers were going on so many strikes that striking became known as the 'British disease'. Why, after the General Strike of 1926, did workers continue to strike on such a large scale? Did the government use the same tactics to deal with striking workers as it had done during the General Strike?

Objectives

- **Examine** the British economy after the Second World War.
- **Describe** the changing relationship between the government and the unions.
- **Explain** the reasons for union failure in the 1980s.

Post-war nationalisation and reform

After the Second World War, there were many changes in British society. There was a strong belief that life should be better for the majority of people; this after all was what people had been fighting for during the war.

The creation of the welfare state, the National Health Service and the nationalisation of key industries were all features of post-war Britain. Nationalisation started with the Bank of England, civil aviation, coal, and cables and wireless. Then came railways, canals, road haulage and trucking, electricity, and gas. The nationalisation of industries played a key role in creating a good relationship between the government, employers and union members. The appointment of Ernest Bevin as a moderate union leader helped to gain union support after the General Strike.

In 1946, the new Labour government passed the Trades Disputes and Trade Unions Act; this amended the same act of 1927. Union membership flourished. This was great news until the 1960s, which brought an increase in prices and a drop in wages.

Industrial disputes: the road to unrest

▼ **A** *Government successes and the fate of the unions*

1960s
Country suffers from periods of inflation; unions demand wage increases to match rising prices

1969
MP Barbara Castle produces a plan calling for a secret ballot and a 28-day cooling-off period before a strike is approved

1969–71
Smaller unions join together; membership continues to increase

1971
Industrial Relations Act introduced: makes ballots compulsory

1972 and 1974
National Union of Miners vote for coal strikes; leads to shortage of coal; government rations electricity and brings in 3-day working week

1974
New Labour government abolishes Industrial Relations Act and introduces social contract instead, securing regular wage increases for workers

1976
Social contract challenged by British-Asian women working in Grunwick Film Processing Laboratories in London; they strike for two years in protest at poor working conditions; their leaders, including Jayaben Desai, go on hunger strike

▼ **SOURCE B** ***Jayaben Desai, picketing during the Grunwick dispute***

Winter 1978–79
Strikes in many industries, leads to 'Winter of Discontent'; reports of rubbish piling up in streets and bodies piling up in morgues as workers strike

1979
Conservatives win election, Margaret Thatcher becomes Prime Minister; government begins to challenge strength of unions

1980 and 1982
Employment Acts introduced, changing rules on picketing and making it unlawful for someone to be dismissed because of a closed shop (a place of work where all employees must belong to the same trade union)

1984
Thatcher's government introduces Trade Union Act; this states 80 per cent of members must agree for strikes to be called; closed shops are illegal unless 85 per cent of workers are happy with situation; secondary picketing (of companies that do business with employer) is outlawed

1984
Miners' strikes, led by Arthur Scargill, sweep country; Women Against Pit Closures set up to rally support in communities and help feed families

▼ **INTERPRETATION C** ***Adapted from an account by a striking miner, John Moulson, in 2015; he remembers what it was like being on the picket line:***

> I lived in a mining town and it was expected that every man would join the picket lines to cause as much disruption to coal movements as possible. It started to get really scary, as not only could we have been seriously injured, we could also have ended up with a criminal record. Throughout the strike the camaraderie between the communities was unbelievable, and the support given by local people enabled many of the miners and their families to survive.

1985
Miners' strike ends in government victory, but the way the miners were dealt with caused controversy. Inflation falls, unemployment rises above 3 million

Laws introduced by Conservatives in early 1980s do not end confrontations between employers and workers; disputes by print industry workers, teachers and miners. None is particularly successful

Huge stockpiles of unsold coal, split in miners' union, well organised policing of pits that continue to work, lack of support from other unions, and negative press attention means miners' strike ends

Industry continues to decline

Extension

In 2014, the film *Pride!* told the story of the LGBT (lesbian, gay, bisexual and transgender) community and their organisation, Lesbian and Gays Support the Miners. Research the impact this group's support had on the miners' strike in 1984.

Work

1. List all the reasons people went on strike in the late twentieth century.
2. Create a graph showing the power struggle between the government and the unions. Put dates along a line, and above put the key events that made the government more powerful in relation to trade unions. Below put the events that made it less powerful.
3. Was the failing economy the main factor, among others, for the failure of the trade unions?

Practice Question

Explain two ways in which the reasons for strikes in the nineteenth century and the reasons for strikes after the Second World War were different. **8 marks**

Study Tip

Try to explain the reasons for each by considering society at the time. Why might one have different reasons from the other? Is it because they had different motivations, or was society different?

12.1 Was the 'mother country' a good mum?

At the beginning of the twentieth century, Britain had a large empire. After the two world wars, many empire countries became independent, some of them keeping ties with Britain by becoming part of the Commonwealth. **Migration** from the Commonwealth helped make Britain the multiracial nation it is today. Why did this migration take place and how did Britain respond to the new arrivals?

Objectives

- **Identify** reasons for immigration to Britain after the Second World War.
- **Describe** the experience of the immigrants.
- **Evaluate** the usefulness of a source about the immigrant experience.

Britain, the mother country

On 22 June 1948, the ship *Empire Windrush* docked at Tilbury, near London. On board were 492 people from the Caribbean. The Caribbean region, like other newly independent countries, was now part of the Commonwealth and had fought for Britain in the First and Second World Wars. In 1948, the British Nationality Act gave all 800 million Commonwealth citizens the chance to come to the 'mother country' and gain full British citizenship. Many decided to take this opportunity. During the 1950s, more people arrived from the Caribbean and from Asia.

Why were immigrants encouraged to come to Britain?

There were many reasons why people from Commonwealth countries were encouraged to come to Britain. Citizenship in Britain was initially awarded to those that had fought alongside Britain in the Second World War. Many other people were keen to take advantage of the British Nationality Act. They had heard so much about Britain and were keen to see the country that had ruled over them for so long. There were also many other reasons why immigrants were encouraged to come.

Loans for transport

It was easy for people to emigrate to Britain: their governments gave out interest-free loans so they could afford the ship fare.

Shortage of labour

There was a shortage of labour for low paid and unskilled jobs in Britain. The British government was trying to rebuild the country after the war, and needed people to fill these jobs. One example is London Transport, which recruited people from Barbados and Jamaica to drive buses and trains. The job opportunities were not always there in their home countries. Furthermore, Britain wanted to secure the loyalty of these countries in case they were needed again.

▶ **SOURCE A** *Men being interviewed during a recruitment fair for London Transport, 1956*

Opportunity

British companies held recruitment fairs like the one in **Source A**. This meant that, before even leaving home, many immigrants had secured a job. The opportunities seemed endless.

▼ **SOURCE B** ***Adapted from a personal account by Arthur Curling, originally from Jamaica, who joined the RAF aged 16:***

> I came to England first in 1944, in the air force. I returned back to Jamaica in 1946. After spending two years there, it was too small for me. But England has something that you want to get back to; you can't put your finger on it.

The immigrant experience

Not everyone shared Arthur Curling's feelings about wanting to be in Britain. The new immigrants were mostly placed in areas where they were needed for work. Early immigrants from the Caribbean were mostly young men, who had planned to make money to send home to their families. This surge of young black men into communities caused some resentment. Most white people moved out to other areas, a reaction called 'white-flight'. In many areas where the white residents remained there was **segregation**. Resentment boiled between young white and black men. Groups of young white men, such as the Teddy Boys, felt that the young immigrants were stealing 'their women'. This tension exploded in 1958 with the Notting Hill Riots in London.

Many immigrants were highly educated but were forced to take low paid, unskilled work, as their qualifications were not recognised in Britain. However, this was not the case for all immigrants. There were many doctors who arrived from the **Indian subcontinent** who were employed in the new National Health Service. The experience of the Asian immigrants was different from those from the Caribbean. Language barriers and religious differences often meant many Asian immigrants formed their own communities and started their own businesses.

Overcrowding was a big problem for all immigrant communities, as many landlords refused to let them rent their accommodation. Local authorities also tried to stop black and Asian people renting houses in particular areas. A high-profile case of this was in Smethwick, Birmingham. The black and Asian residents got the support of Malcolm X, who visited the area in 1965 as a protest against the housing policy towards immigrants.

The British had boasted about their fight against the Nazis in the Second World War. They were proud that they had defeated fascism and racism. However, many groups then experienced discrimination in Britain in the decades that followed. Did Britain, the mother country, really protect all her children?

▼ **SOURCE C** *Malcolm X at Marshall Street in Smethwick, West Midlands, 12 February 1965*

Key Words

migration segregation Indian subcontinent

▼ **SOURCE D** *Racist signs like these encouraged discrimination and hostility towards immigrants*

Work

1 Write out a conversation between a British MP who wants to 'pull' an immigrant to the UK, and an immigrant who explains about the 'push' factors in their home country.

2 a Study **Source B**. What can we learn from it about immigrant experiences?

b Does **Source B** tell us everything about the immigrant experience?

Practice Question

How useful is **Source B** to a historian investigating the immigrant experience in Britain? **8 marks**

Study Tip

Think: the source might not tell us everything, but does it tell us about typical views at the time?

Extension

Find out more about the 1958 Notting Hill Riots. Look at newspaper reports from the time and create a presentation on how the media fuelled discontent in multiracial Britain. Did any media help?

12.2 Did the government make life worse for immigrants?

By 1958, blood had been spilled over immigration. Race riots in Notting Hill and Nottingham resulted in dozens of arrests, many injuries and thousands of pounds' worth of damage. Race relations in some parts of Britain were at a low point. There were clear tensions in society and things were getting worse. The government responded by introducing acts that were meant to improve race relations. What were the aims of these acts? Did they work?

Objectives

- **Outline** the events that led to government controls on immigration.
- **Explain** the key features of the controls.
- **Justify** your opinion about the impact of the immigration controls.

Why was government intervention needed?

After the Notting Hill Riots in 1958, relations between immigrant groups and white residents were not good. Factory owners were increasingly reluctant to employ black workers, and segregation became an even bigger problem in housing, employment and even the social lives of this new community. The general feeling was that too many immigrants were settling in major cities, and that this needed to be stopped.

▼ **A** *Table showing immigration numbers from the Caribbean and from India, Pakistan and Bangladesh*

Year	Caribbean	India, Pakistan and Bangladesh	Total
1956	26,000	8000	34,000
1957	23,000	7000	30,000
1958	17,000	11,000	28,000
1959	20,000	4000	24,000
1960	53,000	10,000	63,000
1961	62,000	50,000	112,000
1962	35,000	47,000	82,000

Government responses

The government had two main aims in responding to the problems. One was to curb the number of immigrants coming into the country; the second was to tackle the racial discrimination that had developed.

The first response was the Commonwealth Immigrants Act, 1962. This controlled the immigration of all Commonwealth passport holders, except the British. It controlled the movement of people by stating that immigrants now needed to apply for a work voucher before they came to Britain. They could only get a voucher if the skills they had were in demand in Britain. This had an effect on many Commonwealth doctors and nurses: they could not find employment in their chosen professions as their qualifications were not recognised.

MPs were divided over Commonwealth immigration controls, but in the 1964 general election those who had been against immigration reform were not re-elected. The people had spoken. They wanted change.

In 1968, another Commonwealth Immigrants Act was passed. This put even tighter controls on immigration, by extending restrictions to those who were part of the Commonwealth but held British passports. If these people did not have a parent or grandparent who was born in, or was a citizen of, the UK, they could not move there. This act confirmed to many immigrants that non-white migration was the problem the government was really trying to stop. The government reforms were perceived as being racist and unfair.

The 1968 act was a reaction to the new politics in Kenya after its independence from Britain in 1963. It had gained independence under Jomo Kenyatta, who had started a policy of Africanisation. Many Asians living in Kenya felt this policy would discriminate against them. Some historians have argued that it was the potential arrival of 200,000 Asians from Kenya that prompted the passing of the Commonwealth Immigrants Act of 1968. It seemed clear that the motivations behind the act were racism and discrimination.

By 1971, the Conservative government was ready to push for even tighter controls, so they passed the Immigration Act. This act replaced employment vouchers with work permits; these permits allowed only temporary residence in Britain. There was also an aspect of the act that encouraged **voluntary repatriation**; this meant the government would assist people in moving back to their country of origin and in changing their citizenship from British to that country. The act still allowed for **chain migration**; this meant families could join those who already had citizenship.

▼ **SOURCE B** *A march in London, 1962, protesting against the Commonwealth Immigrants Act*

Enoch Powell and political opposition

The feeling that these acts were fuelled by racism was further supported in people's minds by politicians such as Enoch Powell. Powell was a Conservative MP in 1968 when Labour was in power. He made a speech which became known as his 'Rivers of Blood' speech, for the way it highlighted the race issue. He said that immigration posed a threat to British identity and that the future would be violent for a multiracial Britain if immigration was not stopped.

▼ **SOURCE C** *Adapted extract from Enoch Powell's 'Rivers of Blood' speech, April 1968:*

> We must be mad, literally mad, as a nation to be permitting the annual inflow of some 50,000 dependants, who are for the most part the material of the future growth of the immigrant-descended population. It is like watching a nation busily engaged in heaping up its own funeral pyre. So insane are we that we actually permit unmarried persons to immigrate for the purpose of founding a family with spouses and fiancés whom they have never seen.

Although his views were shocking, Powell represented a large section of society with similar views. He was not the first politician to try to harness support with these views.

Key Words

voluntary repatriation chain migration second generation

▼ **SOURCE D** *Pro-Powell graffiti, London, May 1968*

With its reactions to immigration, the government had made its views clear. How would the immigrant community respond? What about **second generation** immigrants – people who were actually born in the UK?

Work

1. a Write on cards as many reasons as you can find for the government's controls on immigration.
   b Which reasons show long-term causes of unrest, and which show short-term causes of unrest?
   c Create a table with three columns. These should have the headings: Act; Improving race relations; Supporting the concerns of those against immigration. Provide information about each act, and in the relevant column explain how it either improved relations or supported the concerns.
2. Which act do you consider to be a turning point in immigration control? Use the sources to help you explain your answer. Can you challenge your judgement?

Extension

Research the politics of Idi Amin and his treatment of Asian people in Uganda. Study the government acts again: can you see where the law was changed to help the Asian people trying to escape Amin's rule?

12.3 Protest, riots and reform: how did the people react?

By the early 1970s, the government had done little to reassure the black and Asian communities of Britain that they were equal and welcome. The black community became even more disillusioned when police policies seemed to discriminate against them. By 1981, there had been riots in London, Birmingham and Liverpool. Why did the riots start? How did the government respond? Did relations with black and Asian communities improve?

Objectives

- **Define** Powellism.
- **Explain** the causes of the riots in the UK in the 1970s and 1980s.
- **Evaluate** the significance of immigration to the UK since the Second World War.

Powellism and the National Front

The politics of Enoch Powell received a lot of support, especially from the working class. This support for Powell (known as Powellism) was based on a type of extreme nationalism that viewed white British people as superior to people who were non-white – even if they had been born in Britain.

Some people felt that Powellism fuelled the rise in popularity of a group called the National Front. This group wanted all non-white immigrants to Britain to return to their country of origin – or the country of origin of their parents or grandparents. Many members identified strongly with Hitler's policies in Nazi Germany.

▼ **SOURCE A** *A demonstration against immigration and in support of Enoch Powell, September 1972*

Race Relations Acts

The government introduced some laws that were intended to improve relations between different communities. They would have to reform both society and politics if they were to succeed. The existence of Powellism and the National Front meant the black community would need reassurance that the government represented them as well.

Fact

1965 Race Relations Act: prevented racial discrimination in housing and employment. Seen as a failure due to Race Relations Board bringing no criminal convictions.

1968 Commonwealth Immigrants Act: aimed to help the integration of immigrant communities.

1976 Race Relations Act: extended the definition of discrimination to any practice that disadvantaged another group. Race Relations Board was replaced with the Commission for Racial Equality, which had much greater powers.

▼ **SOURCE B** *Adapted extract from Bernie Grant's archives; Grant was elected MP for Tottenham in 1987, one of only three black MPs at the time:*

> When I arrived here there were still signs on the windows – no black, no Irish, no dogs, no children. Then, there was no Race Relations Act, which outlawed all of that. But what I found was that the problem lay in institutional racism; hidden policies which you found in housing, in education and so on.

Riots: Brixton and the UK

The dream of integration and improved relations was short lived. A year after the 1976 Race Relations Act there was the infamous Battle of Lewisham. This was sparked by a National Front march through the borough. The black community felt let down by the police, as they had allowed the march to happen. Relations between the black community and the police were disintegrating further, as the black community were being blamed for crime in the area. This fuelled the National Front's hatred of the black community further. They claimed, 'a multiracial society is wrong, is evil and we will destroy it.'

▼ SOURCE C *The police clashing with protestors in the Battle of Lewisham, 13 August 1977*

Tensions continued to build, and in 1981 there were riots in Brixton and in other major cities. These riots can be seen as a continuation of the situation in Lewisham, as the role of the police and their poor relations with black communities provided the sparks for the riots. Adding to the tension, the late 1970s was a time of **recession** in the UK. The resulting economic hardships hit black communities the hardest with high unemployment, poor housing and higher crime rates.

Many young black men in Brixton and other immigrant communities felt that they were being discriminated against, despite the 1976 act. This discrimination was due to the law that allowed police to stop and search people they suspected were about to commit a crime – known as the 'sus law'. This law led to what many described as **racial profiling**: they believed black people were being stopped simply because of the colour of their skin. Furthermore, Operation Swamp 81 meant Brixton was filled with plain-clothes police officers from other districts, using 'sus law' as a way to prevent street crime. More than 1000 people were stopped in six days, further increasing tensions as young black men felt attacked in their own community.

Key Words

recession   racial profiling   racially prejudiced

This simmering tension boiled over when rumours of police brutality to a black man led to an angry crowd confronting police officers. The arrest of a young black man on 10 April 1981 saw the start of the riot, where for three days young black people fought the police, and set fire to vehicles and buildings.

The Scarman Report

Lord Scarman was asked to write a report on the events in Brixton. Before his report was published, similar riots had taken place in Handsworth in Birmingham, in Toxteth in Liverpool and in Manchester. The Scarman Report found that institutional racism did not exist within the Metropolitan Police Service. However, the report did suggest making **racially prejudiced** behaviour an offence. The report also led to the end of 'sus law' and the creation of the Police Complaints Authority. These measures improved relations between the police and the black community.

However, in 1993 Stephen Lawrence, a young black man, was murdered in London. It was a racially motivated attack. An investigation showed that the Metropolitan Police Service had not responded appropriately due to institutional racism.

Work

1. **a** Create a graph with a vertical axis showing tension and a horizontal axis showing the years from 1948 to 1981. Plot the events covered on pages 82–87 that caused racial tension in this period.
   b From your graph, which cause seems to be the most common cause of tension?
2. How did the government try to improve race relations?
3. Why was it difficult to improve race relations?

Practice Question

Explain the significance of Caribbean migration to Britain after the Second World War. **8 marks**

Study Tip

You should separate this into short- and long-term significance, and into factors – immigration both influenced politics and changed society.

How to... analyse significance

In your exam, you will have to deal with a question about the significance of something, such as an event, an issue or a person.

Practice Question

Explain the significance of the Peasants' Revolt for the government of Britain. **8 marks**

Study Tip

Judging the significance of a person or events is about looking at their impact on different groups and at different times. Something is significant if it was important at the time *and* is also important today. Even if it only impacted on one group, it can still be significant.

Over to you

When we say an event, idea or person is significant, we mean more than just that it is important. Judging the significance of an event, idea or person is about looking at the impact that it had at the time and how it affected people, and whether it had long-lasting effects or caused important change. You should also consider whether the event, idea or person is still relevant to the present day. Now, work through the following questions.

1. Start by planning out your response: what do you know about the Peasants' Revolt? Try to make notes about what happened in the revolt at the time.
2. Consider the impact of the revolt at the time. Write about how peasants lived and worked before the revolt, and how the revolt was a change compared with what went on before.
3. After you have written about the revolt's impact at the time, move on to consider how it might have an impact in the long term.
4. Lastly, does the Peasants' Revolt directly affect our world today? Remember that the significance of an event, idea or person can change over time, so sometimes a lot of time will need to pass before it is recognised as being significant. Something might not be seen as significant at the time, but years later when more is known, it can be identified as having had a key impact. Equally, something that was significant at the time may lose its significance as a result of later developments, and no longer influences our thinking or world today. So, considering all these points, what do you think is the significance of the Peasants' Revolt?

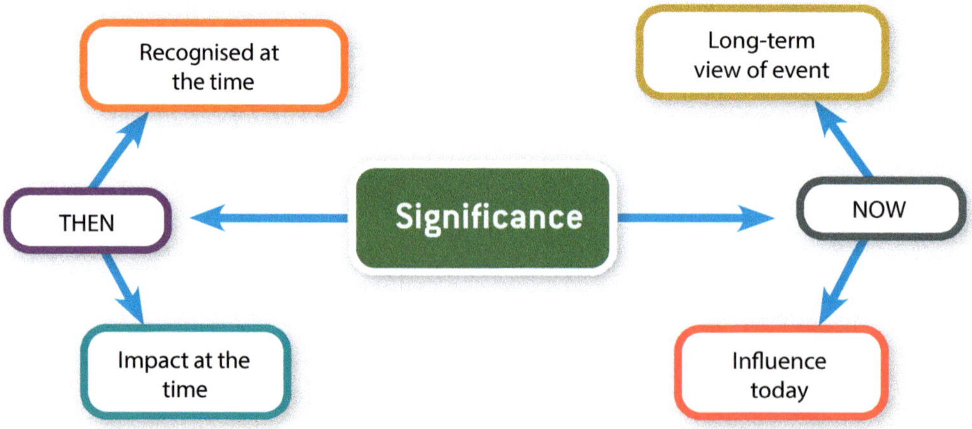

5 Read the following response. Can you identify where the answer explains about the recognition of the Peasants' Revolt, its immediate impact as well as long-term impact, and its relevance today?

The Peasants' Revolt was a great challenge to the king's authority. Medieval kings were used to being challenged by their barons and nobles but not by the peasants. The leader of the revolt, Wat Tyler, was killed by the king and this made him a martyr to many, making him and the revolt significant at the time. The Peasants' Revolt was significant for the government as it showed that the peasants could come together and challenge the king. After the revolt, taxes were never increased, which shows it had an immediate impact.
Parliament did, eventually, stop controlling peasants' wages, which shows the demands of the peasants and the revolt itself were successful.
The government did continue with community charges, so the revolt was not that significant for the government at the time. Another impact of the revolt was that some peasants were able to buy land that was unused after the Black Death. They could no longer be controlled by their landlords and were able to work for themselves. However, this did not apply to all peasants. A hundred years after the revolt, peasants were declared freemen – this is directly linked to the demands of the peasants and shows a long-term impact on society. The Chartists and other movements in the nineteenth century used the Peasants' Revolt as inspiration for their movements, as the revolt challenged the ruling class with some successful outcomes.

6 Now try to answer the Practice Question on page 94 yourself!

How to... analyse sources

In your exam, you will have to deal with a question about the usefulness of a source to a historian studying that particular part of history. You will be asked a question that directly relates to a source.

▼ **SOURCE A** *Drawn in 1649 by Clement Walker, a disgruntled parliamentarian, this is a piece of propaganda called* The Royal Oak of Britain. *Walker was arrested for this drawing and charged with high treason. The drawing shows Cromwell destroying the regime of Charles I.*

Practice Question

Study **Source A**. How useful is **Source A** to a historian studying Cromwell?

8 marks

[Taken from AQA 2016 Paper 2 specimen material]

Study Tip

Ask yourself, 'what is this source?' The provenance (such as the date of publication, the type of source and the title) will help you to assess the usefulness of the source. What do you know about the topic that you can link with the information from the provenance?

Study Tip

The content of the source is the image itself. Begin by describing what you can see. What do you know about Cromwell that you can connect with what you see in the image? Look at what is hanging from the tree.

Over to you

The usefulness of a source is what it tells you about the history of the time. A source might be useful because it reveals something new, why events turned out the way they did, or why people acted or thought in a particular way at that time. This question suggests that the source has a use for historians studying Oliver Cromwell: remember this as you work through the following questions.

1 Start by analysing the content of **Source A**. What is the author trying to say about Cromwell? What does the source tell us about Cromwell that makes it useful or not? The content of the source should be checked against your own knowledge of the topic.

2 You should also consider the provenance of **Source A**:

  a What does it tell you about how useful, or not, the source might be? Provenance could mean who produced the source, why it was produced, who it was produced for, and where and when it was produced. Remember that to answer the usefulness of a source, the provenance of a source is just as important as the content.

  b What was the context of the time in which the source was created? The source dates from 1649, which is the year King Charles was executed. The provenance suggests that it is someone who is unhappy with Cromwell's actions. Perhaps you could argue that this source is useful as it gives evidence that some parliamentarians did not approve of Cromwell as Lord Protector and did not approve of the king's execution.

3 Recall the actual question: it asks about a historian studying Oliver Cromwell. In **Source A** Cromwell is seen to be destroying the 'British Oak' that contains the crown, sceptre and coat of arms; it shows that Cromwell was responsible for destroying the king's rule in Britain. Why might this be? It is helpful if you try to use the provenance and the content together. The provenance says that the person who created this source was a disgruntled parliamentarian. It might seem that he was unhappy with Cromwell. Did all parliamentarians support Cromwell? Was Cromwell responsible for the king's execution?

4 What are the strengths and weaknesses of the following answer?

The source is useful because it comes from the time when the king was executed in 1649 and gives the opinion of someone who fought against the king. It shows that not everyone supported the king's execution and Cromwell as Lord Protector. The source shows Cromwell ordering his men to destroy the British Oak that contains the royal crown. From the branches of the tree hang Magna Carta and the Bible. This shows that the Cromwell was viewed as someone who would destroy the rights of the people who had fought in the civil war and that he was against God. I know that at the time there were many people who were unhappy at Cromwell's influence. They were also worried about the changes he would bring to England. Some people, however, did support Cromwell as he was, despite the drawing, seen as someone who would bring religious toleration after Charles' forced reforms under Laud.

5 Now try to answer the Practice Question on page 94 yourself!

How to... compare similarities

In your exam, you will have to deal with a question about comparing the similarities of two things, such as two events or developments.

Practice Question

Explain two ways in which Magna Carta and the Great Reform Act were similar. **8 marks**

Study Tip

You can explain any aspect of the two events in the question. They may have the same causes but completely different outcomes. It could be that they both have political consequences but one is more significant than the other.

Over to you

This style of question asks you to explain the similarities between two topics or aspects of the history you have studied. You are looking for similarities between the two events: remember this as you work through the following questions.

1. Start by planning out your response: what are the similarities between Magna Carta and the Great Reform Act? Make a list or a mind-map to help you analyse the similarities. For example, when comparing the two events, consider:
   - **a** causes: why did the event happen?
   - **b** development: how did the event develop?
   - **c** consequences: events will have results.
2. Try to organise your response in three sections, covering causes, development and consequences. Remember that you will need to show how well you have understood both events by explaining the similarities that you can find.
3. Read the following response. Can you identify where the answer explains about similarities in terms of causes, development and consequences?

Both events are similar because they were concerned with greater representation. With Magna Carta the barons wanted greater representation in the Great Council, and those campaigning for the Great Reform Act wanted representation in government. The barons were frustrated with King John charging them tax for war and giving jobs to his foreign family; they needed more of a say. Similarly, the middle class in nineteenth-century Britain felt they were not represented as they could not vote for someone who understood their needs. Another way the events are similar is that they did not change life for everyone. Magna Carta gave more power to the Barons, but did not even mention the peasants and villeins. The Great Reform Act could be seen as not that 'great' because it only catered for the middle and merchant class, not the working class. So the events are similar because they were both meant to improve the lives of people by giving them a say but neither helped the poor.

4. Now try to answer the Practice Question on page 94 yourself!

How to... evaluate main factors

In your exam, you will have to deal with a question that asks you to evaluate factors.

Practice Question

Have living standards been the main factor in causing unrest in Britain in the nineteenth and twentieth centuries?

Explain your answer with reference to living standards and other factors.

16 marks

SPaG: 4 marks

Study Tip

Write down all the factors you can think of that caused unrest. Next to each one write the event it links to. Then try to show if some factors influence each other. Once you have completed this you should have a clear idea about which is the main factor.

Over to you

Different factors have affected this power and the people thematic study over a long period of time. Those factors are war, religion, chance, government, communication, the economy, ideas such as equality, democracy and representation, and the role of the individual in encouraging or inhibiting change. Frequently, factors worked together to bring about particular developments at particular times. This question is asking about one particular factor and its influence compared with other factors: remember this as you work through the following questions.

1. Start by writing about the factor that has been named in the question: in this case, it is about living standards. You will have come across examples where living standards have appeared in your study of power and the people. Using these examples, write about how the factor had an influence. The factor you are addressing might sometimes have helped and sometimes have hindered the development of power for the people. Try to give two or three examples from different times or places during your study.
2. Next, consider other factors that have influenced the development of power, for example political representation and race relations. Choose two or three other factors from your study and explain, with examples, how those factors changed the development of power. Again, it is useful if you can find examples from across the wide range of your study that both helped and hindered the development.
3. Lastly, you will have to deal with the judgement in the question. The question picked out that the living standards factor was the main factor. You have to say whether or not you agree with this. Try to weigh up or assess the living standards factor against all the other ones, and say which was more important. To back up your conclusion, you should also explain *why*, with supporting evidence.
4. Read the following essay conclusion to the question. Can you identify: the given factor (living standards) and two other factors? The supporting points about each factor? An assessment or judgement about which is the main factor?

Living standards were an important factor for causing unrest, but they were not the main factor. Although it is true in the last 200 years different groups such as the Tolpuddle Martyrs, the Chartists, the General Strike and the unions of the 1970s all wanted more wages and better working and living conditions, the main factor in causing unrest has been the desire for more representation in government – to have a voice. This is true of the Chartists, the suffragettes and minority groups in the late twentieth century such as the black and Asian communities. All these groups realised that if they wanted to improve their standards of living, they had to have more of a say and therefore more representation in government.

5. Now try to answer the Practice Question on page 94 yourself!

Practice Questions for Paper 2: Britain: Power and the people: c1170 to the present day

The examination questions on the Thematic Studies will be varied but there will be a question on a source (AO3), a question on significance (AO1 and AO2), a similarity/difference question (AO1 and AO2), and an extended writing question using factors (AO1 and AO2). Below is a selection of these different kinds of questions for you to practise.

Answer **all four** questions. You are advised to spend 50 minutes on these four questions.

Source A

A poster printed by suffragettes in 1912. The poster was produced by a group of artists founded in 1909 with the aim 'of encouraging artists to promote the women's movement and particularly votes for women, by means of images'.

1 Study **Source A**.

How useful is **Source A** to a historian studying votes for women?

Explain your answer using **Source A** and your contextual knowledge. **8 marks**

2 Explain the significance of the trial and execution of Charles I for royal authority. **8 marks**

3 Explain two ways in which the campaigns for workers' rights in the nineteenth century and the protests for the rights of ethnic minorities in the twentieth century were similar. **8 marks**

4 Has war and violence been the main way in which royal authority and governments have been challenged?

Explain your answer with reference to war and violence and other ways.

Use examples from your study of Power and the people. **16 marks**

SPaG: 4 marks

Glossary

aristocratic being part of the ruling class or the nobility

autocrat a ruler who holds all the power

autocratic relating to a ruler who holds all the power

ballot slip of paper used to register a vote, completed in secret

baron man who had been given high rank by the king; the title came with land

bills proposed laws presented to parliament for discussion and consideration

burgess person who owned land or a house in a burgh; like peasants they were bound to their lord

catapult device used to launch stone balls or other missiles from far away

catechism fixed questions that are used for religious instruction; common in the Catholic Church

cavalry soldiers on horseback

chain migration process by which immigrants follow family members to a new place; often, laws allow immigrants to reunite with family in the new destination

chancellor in Medieval times this was the person who wrote all the paperwork for new laws and produced other official paperwork

Chartist movement nineteenth-century campaign to gain political representation and rights for working-class people

civil war war between different groups in one country

coal seam bed of coal underground

colonist settler in or inhabitant of a colony

colony country or area under the full or partial control of another country and occupied by settlers from that country

communism political ideology which promotes the common ownership of industry and production with no private owners

Congress national legislative body in the USA that makes laws

crusade religious war fought in the Middle Ages between Christians and Muslims

democracy system of government which gives everyone a say by allowing them to vote for people to represent them in parliament

depression long-term downturn in the economy that can see businesses fail and, in the extreme, people starving

divine right idea that a person (such as a king) has been appointed by God, and has the right to make any decision and not be questioned, as they are God's representative on earth

empire collection of tribes, regions, territories, states or countries that are ruled over and controlled by one leader or 'mother country'; the areas controlled are usually called colonies (although sometimes dominions or dependencies); the mother country makes many of the key decisions to do with the places it rules over

enslaved made a slave; having one's freedom to choose or act taken away

excommunicate officially remove from the Catholic Church by order of the Pope

feudal system Medieval system of land holding and distribution in which the use of the land is paid for by performing services and work for the owner

foreign competition when other countries produce the same product but at a more competitive price or more quickly

free trade trade that is not restricted by governments

freeman peasant in the feudal system who rented land from a landowner for an agreed fee; different from unfree peasants who had to provide services to the landowner in exchange for the land that they used

general strike strike where different industries engage in strike action at the same time

groat silver coin worth four English pennies

guild group of skilled tradespeople who organised pay and conditions

Hundred Years War series of wars between England and France, lasting from 1337 until 1453

indentured servant person who paid for their passage to a new country by signing a contract stating that they would work for a set period of time; indentured servitude was usually voluntary but was sometimes used as a form of punishment

Indian subcontinent large area of land that consists of India, Pakistan and Bangladesh

indigenous American (also known as Native American) person who is a member of any of the first groups of people living in North and South America or the Caribbean

infantry soldiers who fight on foot

inherit gain something from a family member, normally parents; this can be genetic or material, for example money

Justice of the Peace local official appointed by the king, responsible for law and order

knight in the Middle Ages, a man who served his feudal lord as a soldier on horseback

laissez-faire French words meaning 'leave alone'; in the nineteenth century many people felt that this was what the government should do: not interfere, not force people to change, and allow things to take their own course

Laudian something done by William Laud

legislation laws that have been passed by parliament

liberal not as strict and more inclusive of different groups

Maroons a group of formerly enslaved people (and their descendants) who gained their freedom by escaping the plantations to live in a remote location

martyr person who dies for their cause and becomes a symbol for a movement or a cause

mass religious service held by Catholics, led by a priest

merchant person who buys and sells goods

migration the movement of people from one place to another; a person who moves is known as a 'migrant'

militant aggressive and sometimes violent

Model Parliament first parliament to resemble ours today; it had representatives from the Church and the aristocracy as well as those from the counties and boroughs (commoners)

nationalise when the government takes control or owns an industry or a service

occupy take over another country, town or castle; normally used to describe an invading force that takes over a country

orator person who is considered an expert public speaker

pacifist person who is opposed to war and violence

pamphlet small booklet containing information; important during the English Civil War for spreading ideas
and propaganda

pardon act of forgiving a crime

parliament group of people responsible for making laws

peasant person at the bottom of the social structure in feudalism; normally an agricultural worker

penal colony place of imprisonment and punishment at a remote location

peninsula long stretch of land that is connected to the mainland but bordered by water on three sides

petition request to do or change something, normally presented to government; people sign one to show how much support the request has

philanthropist person who donates their time and money to charitable causes

picket to stand outside or near a workplace and try to persuade other workers not to enter the workplace

pilloried when a person is put in a pillory – a wooden frame with spaces for the head and the hands – to be attacked or ridiculed

pious deeply religious, observing religion completely

plantation large farm that specialises in growing usually just one crop

poll tax tax of a certain amount that all individuals over a certain age had to pay, regardless of income

Presbyterian denomination of Protestantism, popular in Scotland

progressive person who is interested in changing politics and modernising society

propaganda literature that is used to promote a point of view; normally used by the government during war

providence God's intervention in the world; people who believe that something is divine providence believe that God wants something to happen

purge physical removal of something or someone; normally carried out violently or abruptly

Puritan hard-line Protestant Christian who believes in simple church services and lifestyles; Puritans protested against the practices of the Catholic Church

racial profiling when police target an individual for a crime, based purely on their race

racially prejudiced discriminating against someone because of their race

radicalism wanting complete political or religious reform

re-nationalise when the government takes over a previously nationalised industry after a period of private ownership

recession period when the economy of a country or the world is poor; this can mean an increase in unemployment

regent person who acts as an adviser to a monarch if they are very young; this person can hold great influence

regicide the killing of a monarch

regulate bring under the control of a law or rule

repeal remove or reverse (a law)

republic country with a system of government where an elected President has supreme power, rather than a monarch

scutage tax collected during wartime; normally paid by a knight instead of completing military service

second generation people who were born in the UK but whose parents were immigrants

segregation deliberate act of keeping groups or communities separate

siege military blockade common in Medieval battles; usually done to starve out an opponent

socialist person believing in the rights of the working class (socialism)

solidarity showing allegiance to a group of people you work with, are the same gender as, or the same class as; working together, not against each other

Star Chamber court where people who had gone against the king were tried; run by supporters of the king

steward person who managed the king's finances and estates; in some cases worked for the king's interests in other countries

strike action stopping work until working conditions improve or demands are met

temperance moderate intake of, or complete abstinence from, alcohol

tenant person who lived on a lord's land and paid rent and taxes; normally a peasant

tenant farmer person who lives and works on land that they do not own, but rent from a landowner

Tory the Tory Party of the nineteenth century believed in a strong Britain and free trade

trade union organised association of workers or skilled tradespeople; they protect the rights of workers and the conditions they work in

trebuchet similar to a catapult; a device used to smash castles and other defences

tyranny when all power belongs to one ruler and treatment is normally cruel and unfair

villein similar to a peasant, person at the bottom of the social structure in feudalism; normally a farm worker

voluntary repatriation returning to the country of origin and gaining citizenship for that country

Whig member of a political party that believed in the power of parliament; the Whig party was important in reforming parliament

Index

Topics available from *Oxford AQA GCSE History*

Germany 1890–1945: Democracy and Dictatorship
Student Book
978 019 837010 9
Kerboodle Book
978 019 837014 7

America 1920–1973: Opportunity and Inequality
Student Book
978 019 841262 5
Kerboodle Book
978 019 841263 2

Conflict and Tension First World War 1894–1918
Student Book
978 019 842900 5
Kerboodle Book
978 019 842901 2

Conflict and Tension: The Inter-War Years 1918–1939
Student Book
978 019 837011 6
Kerboodle Book
978 019 837015 4

Conflict and Tension between East and West 1945–1972
Student Book
978 019 841266 3
Kerboodle Book
978 019 841267 0

Conflict and Tension in Asia 1950–1975
Student Book
978 019 841264 9
Kerboodle Book
978 019 841265 6

Health and the People c1000–Present Day
Student Book
978 138 202310 8
Kerboodle Book
978 138 202312 2

Power and the People c1170–Present Day
Student Book
978 138 202313 9
Kerboodle Book
978 138 202315 3

Migration, Empires and the People c790–Present Day
Student Book
978 138 202307 8
Kerboodle Book
978 138 202309 2

British Depth Studies c1066–1685
Student Book
978 019 837012 3
Kerboodle Book
978 019 837016 1

Time-saving expert support for all 16 AQA options

Teacher Handbook
978 019 837018 5
Professional, practical support filled with subject knowledge, classroom ideas and activities, plus exam advice and support.

Kerboodle Exam Practice and Revision
978 019 837019 2
An online resource packed full of exam practice, revision and continuing timesaving support for the entire specification.

RECAP APPLY REVIEW SUCCEED

Germany 1890–1945 Revision Guide
978 019 842289 1

America 1920–1973: Opportunity and Inequality Revision Guide
978 019 843282 1

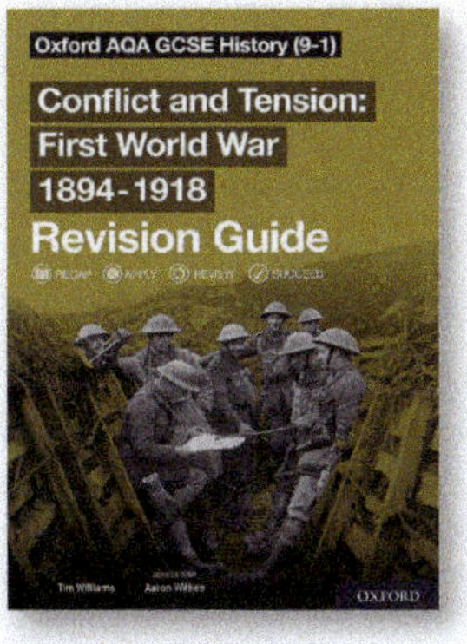

Conflict and Tension First World War 1894–1918 Revision Guide
978 138 200767 2

Give students the confidence to succeed

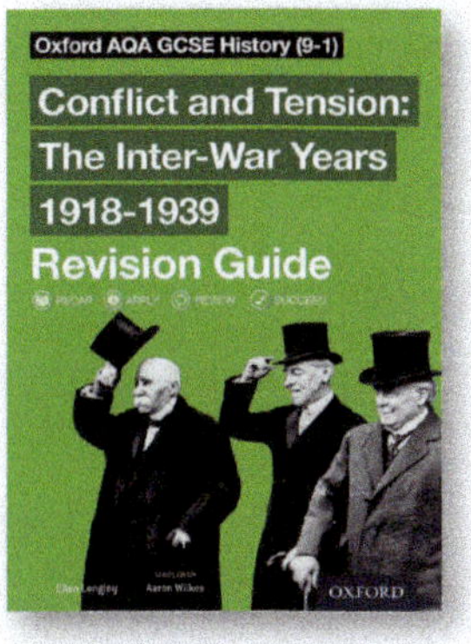

Conflict and Tension: The Inter-War Years 1918–1939 Revision Guide
978 019 842291 4

Conflict and Tension between East and West 1945–1972 Revision Guide
978 019 843288 3

Conflict and Tension in Asia 1950–1975 Revision Guide
978 019 843286 9

Britain: Health and the People c1000–Present Day Revision Guide
978 019 842295 2

Britain: Power and the People c1170–Present Day Revision Guide
978 019 843290 6

Britain: Migration, Empires and the People c790–Present Day Revision Guide
978 138 201503 5

Norman England c1066–c.1100 Revision Guide
978 019 843284 5

Elizabethan England c1568–1603 Revision Guide
978 019 842293 8

All published Student Books have been approved by AQA. The Kerboodle: Exam Practice and Revision, Teacher Handbook, and Revision Guides have not been approved by AQA.

Order online at **www.oxfordsecondary.com/gcsehistory**

Acknowledgements

The publisher and authors would like to thank the following for permission to use photographs and other copyright material:

Cover: World Image Archive / Alamy Stock Photo.

Photos: **p6(tl)**: Walker Art Library / Alamy Stock Photo; **p6(tr)**: Album / Alamy Stock Photo; **p6(br)**: Niday Picture Library / Alamy Stock Photo; **p7(tl)**: Pictorial Press Ltd / Alamy Stock Photo; **p7(br)**: Album / Alamy Stock Photo; **p7(bl)**: Education Images/Universal Images Group via Getty Images; **p7(tr)**: Metropolitan Police Authority/Mary Evans; **p9**: Album / Alamy Stock Photo; **p10**: Walker Art Library / Alamy Stock Photo; **p11(t)**: Mary Evans / The National Archives, London. England.; **p11(b)**: Arcaid Images / Alamy Stock Photo; **p12**: Heritage Image Partnership Ltd / Alamy Stock Photo; **p14**: Mary Evans Picture Library / Alamy Stock Photo; **p15**: INTERFOTO / Alamy Stock Photo; **p16**: Mary Evans Picture Library/DOUGLAS MCCARTHY; **p17**: Bibilothèque Nationale de France; **p18**: Album / Alamy Stock Photo; **p19**: Classic Image / Alamy Stock Photo; **p23**: Chronicle / Alamy Stock Photo; **p24**: Album / Alamy Stock Photo; **p25**: Heritage Image Partnership Ltd / Alamy Stock Photo; **p26(l)**: Peter Horree / Alamy Stock Photo; **p26(r)**: IanDagnall Computing / Alamy Stock Photo; **p28**: His Grace The Duke of Norfolk, Arundel Castle / Bridgeman Images; **p29**: Chronicle / Alamy Stock Photo; **p30(l)**: AC Rider/Shutterstock; **p30(r)**: Private Collection / Bridgeman Images; **p31**: Chronicle / Alamy Stock Photo; **p32**: Niday Picture Library / Alamy Stock Photo; **p33**: Hulton Archive/Getty Images; **p34**: Album / Alamy Stock Photo; **p35**: Chronicle / Alamy Stock Photo; **p37(t)**: Chronicle / Alamy Stock Photo; **p37(m)**: Bridgeman Images; **p37(b)**: Bridgeman Images; **p39(t)**: Chronicle / Alamy Stock Photo; **p39(b)**: Art Collection 2 / Alamy Stock Photo; **p40(l)**: Stocktrek Images, Inc. / Alamy Stock Photo; **p40(r)**: Album / Alamy Stock Photo; **p41**: Rijksmuseum; **p43**: Niday Picture Library / Alamy Stock Photo; **p46**: Chronicle / Alamy Stock Photo; **p47(lt)**: Kaihsui Tai/Wikipedia Commons; **p47(lb)**: Stu / Alamy Stock Photo; **p47(rt)**: Pictorial Press Ltd / Alamy Stock Photo; **p48**: Presented by the Friends of Birmingham Museums & Art Gallery, 1937.; **p49**: National Portrait Gallery, London; **p51**: Chronicle / Alamy Stock Photo; **p52**: Pictorial Press Ltd / Alamy Stock Photo; **p53**: Punch Cartoon Library / TopFoto; **p55**: Granger Historical Picture Archive / Alamy Stock Photo; **p56(l)**: Eric James / Alamy Stock Photo; **p56(r)**: Chronicle / Alamy Stock Photo; **p57**: Everett Collection/Shutterstock; **p58**: Library of Congress, Prints and Photographs Division, Cartoon Prints, British; **p60**: Illustrated London News Ltd/Mary Evans; **p61**: The Print Collector / Alamy Stock Photo; **p65**: World History Archive / Alamy Stock Photo; **p66**: The Print Collector/Print Collector/Getty Images; **p67**: Chronicle / Alamy Stock Photo; **p68**: Pictorial Press Ltd / Alamy Stock Photo; **p69**: University Of Leicester Special Collection (CC BY-NC-ND 2.0 UK); **p70(l)**: Album / Alamy Stock Photo; **p70(r)**: Chronicle / Alamy Stock Photo; **p71(l)**: Chronicle / Alamy Stock Photo; **p71(tr)**: The March of the Women Collection / Mary Evans Picture Library; **p71(br)**: Historic Collection / Alamy Stock Photo; **p72**: National Portrait Gallery, London; **p73(l)**: gameover / Alamy Stock Photo; **p73(r)**: Heritage Image Partnership Ltd / Alamy Stock Photo; **p74**: Heritage Image Partnership Ltd / Alamy Stock Photo; **p75**: Fred W. McDarrah /Getty Images; **p77(bl)**: London Metropolitan University Library Services and Special Collections; **p77(tr)**: Modern Records Office , University of Warwick; **p78(bl)**: Hulton-Deutsch Collection/CORBIS/Corbis via Getty Images; **p78(tr)**: John Frost Newspapers / Alamy Stock Photo; **p78(br)**: John Frost Newspapers/Mary Evans Picture Library; **p79**: Punch Cartoon Library / TopFoto; **p80**: Graham Wood/Evening Standard/Getty Images; **p82**: © TfL from the London Transport Museum collection; **p83(bl)**: Trinity Mirror / Mirrorpix / Alamy Stock Photo; **p83(tr)**: London Metropolitan University Library Services and Special Collections; **p85(l)**: Museum of London/Heritage Images/Getty Images; **p85(r)**: Evening Standard/Getty Images; **p86**: Evening Standard/Getty Images; **p87**: Marx Memorial Library/Mary Evans; **p90**: Library of Congress Prints and Photographs Division Washington, D.C. 20540 USA; **p94**: Pictorial Press Ltd / Alamy Stock Photo.

Artwork by Q2A Media Services Pvt. Ltd.

Although we have made every effort to trace and contact all copyright holders before publication this has not been possible in all cases. If notified, the publisher will rectify any errors or omissions at the earliest opportunity.

Links to third party websites are provided by Oxford in good faith and for information only. Oxford disclaims any responsibility for the materials contained in any third party website referenced in this work.

We are grateful to the authors and publishers for use of extracts from their titles and in particular to the following:

AQA for practice questions from the AQA GCSE History Paper 2 'Shaping the Nation', copyright © 2015 AQA and its licensors. AQA accepts no responsibility for the study tips given which have neither been provided nor approved by AQA.

Cambridge University Press for *Simon de Montfort* by J R Maddicott (Cambridge University Press, 1994).

Curtis Brown Group Ltd, London on behalf of The Estate of C L R James for *The Black Jacobins* by C L R James (Secker & Warburg, 1963), copyright © C L R James 1938.

Oxford University Press for *English History 1914-1945* by A J P Taylor (OUP, 1992), first published in *The Oxford History of England* (1965).

UK Parliament: Simon de Montfort's Parliament, from 'The Provisions of Oxford', https://www.parliament.uk/about/living-heritage/evolutionofparliament/originsofparliament/birthofparliament/overview/simondemontfort/provisionsoxford, is Parliamentary information licensed under the Open Parliament License v3.0

We have made every effort to trace and contact all copyright holders before publication, but if notified of any errors or omissions, the publisher will be happy to rectify these at the earliest opportunity.